Until Further Notice,
I Am Alive

Until Further Notice, I Am Alive

I Am Alive

Tom Lubbock

GRANTA

Granta Publications, 12 Addison Avenue, London W11 4QR

First published in Great Britain by Granta Books, 2012

Copyright © The Estate of Tom Lubbock, 2012
Introduction copyright © Marion Coutts, 2012

Extract from a letter sent by William Empson, from *Selected Letters of William
Empson*, ed. John Haffenden (Oxford University Press, 2006), first published
in *Critical Quarterly*, Volume 6, issue 1, pp. 83–4 in March 1964.

Lines from the 'Aria of the Falling Body' from *The Death of Klinghoffer*
reproduced by kind permission of Alice Goodman.

Lines from *Bully for Brontosaurus: Reflections in Natural History* by
Stephen Jay Gould. Copyright © 1991 by Stephen Jay Gould.
Used by permission of W. W. Norton & Company Inc.

A CIP catalogue record for this book
is available from the British Library.

1 3 5 7 9 10 8 6 4 2

ISBN 978 1 84708 531 3

Typeset by M Rules
Printed and bound by CPI Group (UK) Ltd, Croydon, CR0 4YY

Contents

Introduction
by Marion Coutts

Tom wrote this book. That in itself is astonishing.

Tom was my husband. Writing was his life and work. But in September 2008 he was diagnosed with a Grade Four brain tumour, situated in the left temporal lobe, the area responsible for speech and language. The progression of the tumour and the writing of this book happened over the same time. During his last year, articulate speech became an effort. He willed words into being as they vanished again. It was a transcendent time, volatile and strange; full of danger. Tom's work was to keep his illness and his life in clear sight. His task was, in his own words, 'a lesson in imagination, in self-imagination'. The incredible thing was that he could write this down.

Until Further Notice, I Am Alive brings two texts back together, one long and one short, one pulled from the other.

1

The bulk of the work was an extended and private piece of writing, a journal Tom kept between his diagnosis and the time he could no longer work unaided in September 2010. The journal was provisionally titled *The Present Crisis*, and its last dated entry is 26 August 2010. After that, his energy went into a 5,000-word article commissioned by the *Observer* about his illness, speech and the written word, constructed even as his language collapsed. This was a mixture of new writing and material from the journal. The article was published as 'When Words Failed Me' on 7 November 2010.

Our house had long been a word factory. Since 11 a.m. on 11 March 2010, when we noticed Tom's words skip their sense in a more radical way, we knew that we were really in trouble. Tom had a second craniotomy on 13 April. After this, we were focused on the making of meaning. The level of production was intense. Tom kept writing. He revised older texts, collated essays, organised his ideas, worked on images for an exhibition and wrote new material.

Tom's initial draft of the *Observer* article was edited with two friends, Jenny Turner and Tim Hodgkinson, throughout October. Time was pressing. Tom's speech was now wayward in the extreme. It had patterns we thought we were getting used to which would snarl themselves up or evolve over days into new ones. It was vertiginous. Vast holes in language would suddenly appear, and great chunks of speech fall away. He strung words together like ropes across voids. I could always understand him, just. At a certain point I became his mouthpiece, although without being his brain I was a fraud.

By October 2010, Tom could not write or read in any regular sense although he could comprehend text on a mysterious level, often after the fact. Yet he was lucid to the last in what he wanted to say. Our job was to help him say it. All 357 words of the last section of the article – which make up the last section of this book – were understood, spoken aloud and pulled together through question and answer, repetition, verbal challenges, inspired guesswork and frustration. With language, Tom was a master improviser. That his intellect and identity were preserved was a matter of chance. Under pressure, his brain was a miracle of plasticity: ever adaptive, patient, persistent.

Once the *Observer* article was published, work continued on the main body of this book. Jenny Turner read aloud every word of his journal to him for his approval on the eighth floor of Guy's Hospital in a communal ward, during visiting hours, two till eight.

If you only knew of Tom through his journalism, you would never have known he was ill. For two years after his diagnosis, he kept up his normal output for the *Independent* – two pieces of work a week, of roughly 1,500 and 1,000 words. Often there was more: collages and other writing. He remained fully engaged with the world, travelling, reading, looking at artwork and exhibitions, thinking about them and making sense of them. The getting of things exactly right with words was his job of many years' standing; his pride. These public communications were now hard-fought; they took double, nearly triple the time to write, and consumed more energy to compose than I can describe. Our house kept no hours, and Tom worked later and later into the night. On 13 September 2010, he filed one of his last pieces, on Carpaccio's *St Augustine in His Study*; the saint turning to the window, the little dog following his gaze.

I met Tom at a friend's kitchen table in 1996. Our work was close and divergent: me an artist, he a writer about art, a critic and an illustrator who worked with images, creating the collages which appeared weekly between 1999 and 2004 on the editorial page of the *Independent*, and intermittently since then. We married in 2001, and Eugene was born in 2007. At the time of his diagnosis we were three; a man, a woman and a young child. We had not always lived like this. We married late, and had the child late. We knew what it was like not to live like this. But however much we had relished our lives previously, we liked this one more. Of all the couples we knew, we spent the most time in each other's company. We thought each other was the best there was.

In illness, Tom's appetite for food and friends became gargantuan. The need for food was drug-fuelled, and his desire for friends was an intensification of the way we liked to live. Talking and words was the whole of our work; all we ever did, really. When communicating became a strain, he had to run at it to get into mode and voice – as if he had to warm up. The more he talked, the better he got. Talking was a high-stakes struggle. When he got going, he was very, very good, until fatigue set in. Even without words he could be funny, his face a mobile comedy. Yet occasionally there were times when Tom could speak when we had nothing more to say. It was a luxury then to sit next to each other in silence.

A palliative nurse came to see us at home in the autumn of 2010. She said, 'On a scale of one to seven, how would you rate your quality of life?' There was a long pause while we digested this madness. Tom, slightly absent, lightly bored, said thoughtfully, 'That is a ridiculous question. Obviously we go – "Oh God," all the time, at all the stuff to be done. But, generally, it is wonderful. We are interested.'

Tom's illness was our disaster and our adventure. He wrote, 'Whatever, there'll be something new.' But there was already something new. Our child was only eighteen months old when Tom was diagnosed, and alongside this journal runs the other narrative of Eugene. Tom and Eugene's stories are intertwined as tight as you can imagine. In normal circumstances, a child's story between eighteen months and nearing four is dramatic enough, one of sudden bursts and huge departures casually taken in their stride, a growing-up story, a getting-to-grips-with-language story. His father's illness was the whole of his nascent experience, and Eugene's understanding of it developed as he grew. He was spared the sudden violence of knowledge. All the rest he experienced with us. Nothing was hidden from him. He was at the centre of everything, one of three, his operations whirring in and out and all around our edges.

Tom went into Guy's Hospital on 30 October 2010. Over the previous six days I had seen something fall away from him each day. He was losing mobility on his right side, and could no longer walk or hold his weight upright. We live in a tall house with thirty-eight stairs, twenty-three of them to reach the main living space alone. Those six days, from a Monday to a Saturday, signalled the end of home. Just after his diagnosis two years earlier he had written, 'Of course I am helpless. And so what do I do with helplessness?' The answer was – a great deal. The momentum we had built up carried us on. Our only guide was the sense of the time we had; the rest was up for grabs.

There were many things to celebrate in the last two months of Tom's life. On 7 November 2010, his article was published in the *Observer*, its cover image showing Tom and Eugene sitting on the grass, like big and little versions of each other. On the sixteenth we heard the news that *Great Works*, his essay anthology, would be published. Then suddenly, on 7 December, we were sprung from our provisional camp at the hospital into Trinity Hospice. This was liberation. We three could live together again. On 9 December, Tom was guest of honour at the party to celebrate the opening of an exhibition of his collage works at the Victoria Miro gallery. Then came Christmas, with Eugene opening too many presents among many friends. Tom's birthday on 28 December meant another party, with soup and singing and champagne. At New Year, we were out on the common in the chill air. We had less than two short winter days with no speech at all. On 9 January 2011, he died.

Moving into Trinity Hospice provided us with a future that lasted thirty-four days. I can only write this piece because I have had that future, and the nature of it allows me to turn and look back. Normally, the experience of love is continuous with daily life, giving it shade and colour, and the everyday goes on illuminated by it. For us, the substance of the quotidian had fallen away. Everything came down to the experience and the actions of love. This felt not like shrinking but expanding. It filled all space. Here we were tighter, denser, more saturated in each other than we ever were before.

Death is personal; it turns eyes inward. Tom was no exception, but you will sense from his writing that we were not alone. Dying happens in the world, and our instinct from the start was towards the social and the public. Organising the exhibition and writing the *Observer* article were loud manifestations of this instinct, but since Tom's diagnosis we had also been sending an email list round to friends and relatives, a condensed bulletin of our lives that went dormant when things were good and flared up when the news was bad. There were not so many emails – twenty-one – between September 2008 and January 2011. They all started with the phrase *Dear Friends*. There were many friends. Their names are not all written here, but they fill out the background of this book. Everything that is described in it happened in the arena they made around us. They gave their time, their ingenuity, their skills, their love and their attention.

We were the lay people orbiting about him. Then there were the professionals. Tom's care was exquisite and complex – and all on the NHS. It happened at four sites across London: The National Hospital for Neurology and Neuro-surgery at Queen Square; St Thomas's Hospital; the Hedley Atkins ward in Guy's Hospital and Trinity Hospice. At the apex were the consultants. His triumvirate of care was the oncologist Dr Lucy Brazil, the neurosurgeon Mr Neil Kitchen and the neurologist Dr Robin Howard.

People would say to me, 'What a nightmare, I don't know how you are coping ...' or many variations on this. I would say, or sometimes too tired to speak, just think – *But this is the good bit. He is still here.* If it did chance to come out of my mouth, I could see that they often did not believe me.

I was right. His loss is a daily outrage. But the manner of

his going was something else, something I haven't yet worked out. I knew that his mind could handle everything that was thrown at it. That his dying would be so exactly continuous with his living, one and the same, was not something I understood in advance. I had thought that death was a separate, foreign state. It is, but it follows the contours of our own terrain. What we needed to know here was an extension of what we knew already. It was not even strange. And because we knew this terrain so intimately, we were able to continue on through it as allies. Very early on, Tom wrote: 'The shape of the creature is the pressure of life against the limit of death'. We were right against the limit for a very long time, and we knew what we were doing and we kept on doing it. During that long time something was made, and here it is.

A Piece of News

August 2008

The news was death. And it wasn't going to be maybe good luck and getting through it. It was definitely death, and quite soon, meaning a few years. And at first, it didn't seem too bad.

I woke up in Ipswich Hospital, coming round in gradual stages of waking and sleeping, and with slowly diminishing grogginess, so that when I was awake enough to see where I was, I was already used to being there, and anyway I hadn't enough clarity of mind to see how surprising my new situation was. I had no shock at this initial turn of events – at why I was not in bed with my wife in the house of the friends we were staying with in Suffolk. I remembered nothing of the fits I'd had in the middle of the night, or being stretcher-chaired down the steep stairs, or ambulanced to the desolate out-of-

11

town hospital. They thought it was a small stroke, at first.

A similar process saw me through the appointments, tests and phone calls of the next 10 days or so, back in London: the GP, St Thomas's. I was still spacey, dreamy. I was already in the midst of the crisis, and open to its possibilities, before becoming fully alive to it. There was never a moment of catastrophe. There was not much waiting, either. Things happened faster than I'd expected. The first meeting with the neurologist was followed at once by the MRI scan of my head. The results came the next day. I found it quite easy to accept the neurologist telling me that the scans were with him, and that they showed a mass, a small tumour in the left temporal lobe, which was in all probability, given its shape and position, malignant, though whether it was primary or secondary he had no clear view. I found it easy to accept that this was being told to me on the phone, and on my mobile. I was at home, as it happens, but I might have been anywhere. I found it all very easy to accept.

'Behold, I shew you a mystery ...' No souls without bodies.

Mortal. We occupy a limited patch of space (I have never believed in travel) for a limited stretch of time. Like the art of realistic painting: pictures hold an equivalent in the confined areas which they enframe, and the brief narratives or actions they represent. Others think paintings figure mortality through paint itself. Perishing, like flesh. Manipulated by our failing bodies.

We know the deal. We're bodies. We are not in our own hands.

4 September 2008

Marion (suddenly, after gasping, weeping, as we're walking along): OK. I'm on it.

Why am I calm? Why have I been walking around with Marion today feeling kind of blessed? Ever since the attack 10 days ago I've seemed to be in a new life. That I didn't die then, and since then am standing on the surface of the earth as on a stage. The tumour diagnosis has only made that state of mind firmer. I'm very open to sadness. As yet, not to fear – though unspeakable running fear was always what I imagined. What can harm me?

But I also connect this gaiety to the materialism of Poussin: 'I'd like a term for "confidence in the world", snakes and all ...' (T. J. Clark in his Poussin book).

And then I think of Eugene and his 'Sssss's' – meaning snakes, and letter S's, and *sss* noises, and any long and wiggly-shaped thing – learning the connectedness of object, word, sound, shape, mark; the basics of learning, before yet learning to distinguish, say, sign connection from simile connection.

I'm very open to sadness now. (How much of E's life will I see?) Very open to being moved. (By words, music, by a sense of my own pathos and the pathos of the situation.) I'm not yet open to fears, or depression. Disbelief so far? Hysterical elation? Wait. Be careful with the hares of hopes and fears. Have patience with yourself. Have mercy on yourself.

Eugene will be OK. Marion will be OK.

9 September 2008

To Jenny Polak, email:

'I have a piece of news I think you ought to know. A very small tumour has been detected in my brain, described, on the basis of an MRI scan, as the size of a peanut and peripheral, on the left temporal lobe. It's not certain, but possible from its position and look, that it's malignant. At any rate, it will need to be removed, and seems to be removable. Of course there may be more wrong with me, but that's what we know so far.

'The beginning of this story is that two weeks ago, in the middle of the night, I had some fits, caused it now seems by a small bleed from this tumour. I woke up in Ipswich Hospital (we were staying with friends near there) and was discharged the same day. It was viewed at the time as a small stroke. After the first day I was basically OK. It was at this point, incidentally, that I sent you my previous message.

'I'm perfectly well at the moment, and feeling well looked after by the neurology department at St Thomas's. I must not predict my state of mind as the situation continues and develops, but as things stand I am calm, focused and even energised by this condition of life, which was not at all how I ever expected to react. Perhaps I hadn't reckoned with having Marion and Eugene; I don't understand it really, but ever since my attack I have understood that I am in a new life, where anything is possible.

'I'm waiting to hear tomorrow what a panel of experts think should be the next step. I am not telling many people at the moment, partly because the situation isn't yet clear, partly from professional prudence, partly because I don't want to have the same conversation over and over. I have told Martha, but otherwise keep this to yourself. I will of course keep you up with developments.'

Telling friends. I have always been very bad with others' afflictions. How to help them not to be so bad with mine? Or who is cheering who up? The business of cheering oneself up, keeping a balance, so as not to be too downcast now, and yet not even more downcast later. Keeping openness.

The time after: when I won't be here, but other people and things I know will. For instance, the sofa bed we bought, which was delivered that same day the scan news came. The time until, that must be filled with, among other matters, contingencies, quite unspecial things, wastes of time. Wherever the division between these two times should happen to fall. For that sofa bed, which seems very well made, will likely outlive me, however long I live. And these outlivers and fillers may be befriended. Household gods.

I thought fear at the idea of my non-existence would seize me. I find it's sadness at the idea of loss, parting, those I love, the world, that pierces me. I am moved by praise of the world. (There's a bit of Haydn's *Creation* on the radio, finale, 'Vollendet ist das grosse Werk'; a very untranscendental work, which tries to elide the Fall; and even the 'Representation of Chaos' is glorious.) I have no desire so far for the lifeboat of immortality. The goodness of the world is all I know or can imagine or wish for.

We are bodies. They go wrong. We mustn't throw up our hands before this well-known fact. At the moment the

16

goodness of earthly life is very present to me – not only in goodbye mode, simply in my heightened awareness of being a body. But it helps, very much helps, at this point, that I don't feel ill at all, and that I'm not expecting to be ripped up.

It is natural to look for divine help. Prayers mainly say 'help'. Do I sense the presence of Jesus, offering me his hand? He is my native god, and I wouldn't be surprised. But whatever help he offers, the deal is, I have to want above all to live in Jesus-land. But I want to live, if any-where, here.

About abandoning: what one will never do again. But how much is already gone? All your childhood, youth. And to feel that you can recover these losses through transporting memory can be as an escape from the losing game.

One is never surprised to find that one is not dead. Though others may be, very.

I keep feeling: I am blessed. By this change of life, I am blessed. How long for? Till what news or outcome or wearing down?

Consolation of animalism: we are animals, we are oper-ating systems, simple economies of need, pleasure, pain, energy, misfortune; this brings relief from our larger griefs, losses. Keats in a letter: 'I go among the Fields and catch a glimpse of a Stoat or a fieldmouse peeping out of the withered grass – the creature hath a purpose and its eyes are bright with it. I go amongst the buildings of a city and I see a Man hurrying along – to what? The creature hath a purpose and his eyes are bright with it.'

One blessing at the moment: being let off from having to think about the future; from making plans, projects; I can't be required to look more than a few weeks ahead, and now being relieved of it, see what a pressure future-mindedness (albeit coming to nothing mostly) usually exerts; and then, being relieved of it, you find you're in a more productive state of mind.

I try to predict nothing, stay open to all possibilities, stay steady. Not only to protect myself and others from torment – the frenzy or paralysis of anxiety – but also as a state of mind that will serve me best.

Of course I am helpless. And so what do I do with helplessness?

I always felt from the start that it would be wrong to complain, to protest, to be outraged, to say (or to agree) what a bummer, what a fuck, wrong even almost to treat the situation as an evil at all – even though of course I would be so glad to be out of it. It is partly an acceptance of the human state. This is one of the ways we go wrong. It is partly a kind of self-respect. This going wrong is the way *I* have gone wrong. I will not deny it, abjure it.

People in my state, neither well nor dying, are in a halfway house of life, inherently transitional, difficult to deal with (a standing reproach to the well, a bringer of danger, bad news, the living moribund – this is essentially the wicked magic of cancer); one could wish that we went away, were put out of circulation, until the matter had been decided one way or the other – and we were either back in the land of the living, or certainly headed for the grave. But it is elementary wisdom – not really granted me till now – to see that this halfway house is a common state of life, which any of us may find ourselves in, and therefore must find ways of living in, and find ways of living in with others. The dying are another class again; the permanently but stably disabled, the chronically sick, another again.

'You'll be hearing on . . .' These delays, these puttings on hold: a mixed blessing. They allow you to relax, to have a few days of reprieve, before the next stage of knowledge, before the process begins again; but at the same time, to come out of the state of readiness, to defocus, almost to imagine that the thing isn't happening, hasn't happened, which is dangerous.

*

A seizure; a caesura; a line drawn through my life.

I'm taken by that idea, when not in trepidation; the idea that, whatever, there'll be something new.

18 September 2008

Meeting the surgeon.

On the scan I thought it looked like a full stop, or a gob-stopper. The Ipswich doctor said: I can assure you there's no tumour. The neurologist at St Thomas's said: it's the size of a peanut. The surgeon at Queen Square said: a bit bigger than a peanut! – pointing to something the size of, I suppose, a bigger marble or grape.

I'm trying to be an accepter of – not fate – but the condition of being a body in all its ways. Feeling attracted to the level, the steady, the undramatic. The prosaic, material, solid, opaque, secular, untranscendent, this-worldly. Art that holds to things, to talk, to the useful and functional, to bodily and social gestures. Empson's poems. Brecht/Weill. Léger. The opaque, not the transparent.

Fear of losing language: this is really the only thing that's consuming me. I can't imagine how it would go.

At the moment: the feeling of absolute helplessness; or at any rate, the acceptance of the fact – since I don't always feel it. And this feeling or acceptance is likely to attract a religious language: I mean, an instinctive prayer of self-committal into the hands of ... I felt one coming up out of me a few days ago – even though the thoughts and feelings that have sustained me so far have been resolutely, defiantly secular (in so far as one can tell the difference). But one is in the end helpless, and what is a secular language for that?

I don't always feel it: meaning that the odd thing about this affliction is that for me, now, it's wholly a matter of knowledge and how I deal with this knowledge; I'm not suffering in body at all, the fits I didn't know about, I'm extremely well, there's nothing I want rid of or treated, except this thing that I know about, and perhaps some more things that I don't yet know about. So the dangers of the disease and of the treatment present themselves in an intellectual way. My helplessness is a fact; I see it, I accept it, but it's unaccompanied and unsupported by any symptoms of bodily helplessness. I can't feel: I'm a crock, I need making better, I'm already helpless in that way, so putting myself helplessly in the hands of medicine and its risks is only to pass from a bad master to a good. No: I'm a free man, submitting to this, for what I recognise is my own good. But the fact also is, however well the operation goes, I will certainly feel much worse after it than before.

What I'd thought was: this kind of experience was

transcendental. 'Crossing the frontier ...' I thought it took you out of communication, beyond all the sense you'd previously learned. You would be left speechless, resourceless, without any grasp upon it. And to others you may well seem out of communication. 'What can you say?' Well, there's a question of what you can decently say, all sorts of opportunities for the wrong tone, the wrong tack. But there is in fact plenty to say, and it is conversant with what there is to say anyway. There is a continuity. Strangely, what you knew already applies, even though there are, as always, new things to learn as well.

I should mention this. Two or maybe three times since my attack, once just now, Friday morning, I have experienced an episode of what I would describe as word-blindness or deafness. They last a few minutes. It is hard, in the nature of it, to follow and record what specifically happens in these quite short periods. It's as if I've become very remote and detached from words. I'm no longer fluent. I've forgotten how to do it. I can't do it automatically. I can't hear whether a word that I say has come out right or not. It's as if it's not me that's speaking, but some kind of inefficient proxy forming the words. It's like there is a time delay between speaking and hearing your own words, or as if you were speaking a language whose phonetics and semantics you didn't properly know. And when I speak or write, the words do sometimes come out wrong, slightly nonsensically. Though, NB, I'm not sure that syntax is similarly affected.

To test myself, I read aloud a passage that I'd just written in an article. There were probably several glitches, but I could only pin down one. When I read these words '... floating and flailing weightlessly', I said the word 'weightlessly' as 'walterkly'. It took quite a bit of effort to be fully sure that it was a mistake; and more effort and repeating to grasp what exactly this nonsense word was, to establish its sound – I had to construct it phoneme by phoneme – clearly enough to write it down. And it seems that the reading eye, darting backwards and forwards, was plucking letters from the whole vicinity, and mixing them up, having lost its usual ability to sort them. One does make this kind of mistake in the normal way, but one also spots it and corrects it swiftly, and this I could not do.

What the whole thing emphasises, of course, is how what we call self-command is really a matter of having reliable automatic mechanisms, unthinking habits or instincts.

But now I can't be certain this wasn't an episode of self-generated panic.

Brain surgery: I'm not worried about the operation itself; no, what an amazing thing; I'm feeling excited, honoured, to be benefiting from, taking part in, human expertise at this high level.

*

On the high-dive. Marion said today, Sunday, what an extraordinary time this is, simply waiting for it to start, not knowing what will happen, going into it voluntarily.

Operation 1

29 September 2008

We go into hospital in the middle of the day, waiting for the whole of Monday morning for the appointment to be confirmed. Trying to find something to do in hospital. Trying to get into bed, or sit on the bed, to find a role in the sick place, still feeling very well.

I'm prepared for being in hospital, I'm given my gown. A rather reluctant nurse tells me she has to take swabs from three or four parts of my body, one of which proved hard to specify; turns out to be not the anus itself, but the area of skin between the scrotum and the anus. She takes them. Shortly afterwards, she comes back and says that two of them have to be taken again.

'Why?'

'They were spoiled.'

'Did you drop them?'

'Yes.'

This is the beginning of a bad relationship.

I am to be the first operation the next morning. This is good. Knobs are attached to my head, to guide the equipment. A Stealth MRI scan. Marion leaves. I'm trying to make precautions against the remote possibility of death or total mental incapacity. Writing messages. Going into tears as I imagine the future when I won't be there – I mean, when I think of Marion and Eugene, of him having no memory of me at all later in life. I lie up writing quite late.

I wrote to Marion:

'Marion, all my love to you, and all my praise to you. Once, when we hardly knew each other, sitting in the kitchen in 46 Spenser Road – I don't think we were even alone – you said, I can't remember about who or what: "You don't want *her*, you want a round-headed lass." Meaning you. And the strangeness and directness of the phrase really took me. You were entirely right. That was what I wanted, and have, and still want. Of course, I don't really believe I will die or lose my mind tomorrow. But with the smallest chance – I wouldn't want to leave you without telling you how delightful, how wise, how kind you are. I've often wondered about the unfathomable process that made you; wondered, when did she learn this, where did she pick that up? – wondered, because you seemed to have a sureness that I felt to have been there from the beginning; though it must have been a formation out of many lessons, experiences, decisions. And recently I've tried to apply these thoughts to Eugene, to his mysterious unfolding. How sure I am that you and he, together and in your individual selves, will go on well. I wish I were with you both, to see this and take part in this. What a fantastic pleasure it's been so far. Dearest Marion, dearest wife, Eugene's mother, enormous gratitude and love and good wishes to you. What was the phrase? Best regards, Tom.'

To Eugene I wrote:

'Darling Eugene,
Nobody remembers anything before they were two. You won't remember me. And I don't have much idea about who you are – or who you will be, at the age at which you'll be able to understand this letter. I'm already beginning to feel that I don't quite understand you. I never imagined you would be very much like me. But I did often imagine going out with you, going to see things, walking and talking, asking questions, making jokes, having arguments. In the last few weeks, just as Marion and I have been getting this news about my brain tumour, you've been picking up language so fast. The little chats we have in your bedroom, when you wake up at 6 a.m., and I go in, and you're standing in your cot, pointing something out that's taken your

27

interest: it's a great moment in the day. And this morning Marion made a film of us having breakfast. She played it back to you. You looked at the red car in your hand, and the same red car you were holding in your hand in the film, and said: "Same".

'As I'm writing this, I'm fully expecting to survive this operation. But there's a very small chance I won't survive, and so I thought I should have a message ready. I grew up without a father. It can be done. It would have been much better if we'd had more years together. But knowing you, at one and a half, I feel that whatever happens you'll be OK. I want to praise you for being a wonderful baby. Well, that's all I know about you. You have done everything well, so far. Go on. I never thought I'd have a child. And then, when you were going to be born, I was frightened at the thought. But when you were born it seemed as if you'd always been with us. Go ahead, Eugene, my only child. Whatever you're doing, I love you. I so strongly hope you'll never have to read this message, or if you do, I'll be alive and reading it next to you. But now, not knowing the future, I say goodbye to you, I kiss you, all my love, Dad.'

Then I sleep well. I always sleep well at this time. I wake up quite early – at the usual time for Eugene's waking. Marion and Eugene arrive at seven. It's a mistake to bring him in: the place, my look, too weird. He freaks out.

*

The hour approaches. Mr Kitchen appears, in a suit and a silvery tie, beaming.

'Good morning, Mr Lubbock.'

'Good Morning, Mr Kitchen.'

'Are we ready for the off?'

'I think so.'

Some more Qs and As.

'So we're ready to go?'

'I'm surprised you dress so well for the occasion.'

'We're looking after you.' (Squeeze of hand.)

I'm taken down in the gown, two floors, cold, in the lift. One anteroom, then another room for the anaesthetic. It looks like a storeroom, a box room, notices stuck up written in marker pen, saying don't do this and that. They want you to go out not realising that it's happening, keeping you distracted. I want to have some kind of last word. 'Now we're putting some water in, just to open up the veins – you'll feel a little water – what do you do? – that must be very interesting.' But I'm saying: 'And am I about to lose consciousness now?' 'Yes, very soon now.' And you feel the amazing speed at which your consciousness drains away, not quite so fast that you can't follow it, but fast and steady and blissful, just enough time to say: Goodbye everybody (though there were only two of them).

The bliss of waking in recovery. My fingers work. All my mobility seems to work. My mind is working. I can speak, and our greatest fears are allayed. Though speech problems will emerge as the days pass, at first I'm just aware of the gradually increasing capability. I lie in bed, trying to recall poems that I know by heart. They materialise bit by bit. A line I couldn't bring to mind suddenly returns some hours later.

Mr Kitchen appears: 'All marbles there?'

It is a tumour. The tumour seems to originate from the brain, not a secondary. To Marion he says: it's a glioma, which indicates it's malignant. Later he says: there are no benign tumours, really – just more or less active growers.

Euphoria. Many visitors, too many. Much talking. I'm up and about in a day or two. I'm becoming aware of speech problems, and these seem to get slightly worse, though the level fluctuates. But generally now I'm imagining a full recovery – and then imagining how I would feel about the preceding. Trying to hold in balance the foreboding before and the relief after; not letting the present wipe out the past – as we said to each other, a few days before, we must not forget this time.

I don't feel sure now, after this emergence and relief, I'm ready or steady for all the bad possibilities. I'm on a roll. I believe that I will escape the worse outcomes. I know that I may need to struggle more. But at the moment, I'm not open to everything. Simply getting through the operation has made it harder to prepare for the next news. If the biopsy news had come with the coming round, if everything was told at once, that might be better. But relief and growing strength is allowed to set in – then we wait for the results.

Good weather. Walks round the square. 'How beauteous mankind is.' We get home on the Friday, in a taxi with our friend Tim. I don't have too much memory of how I lived in the first days and weeks. Again, many visitors, and very exciting talking. The first fits. (They weren't giving me any steroids.)

My dysphasic behaviour.

Charles Péguy: *'A word is not the same with one writer as with another. One tears it from his guts. The other pulls it out of his overcoat pocket.'*

Following my operation, there are occasional losses of speech.

The lines go down for a few minutes, or for longer episodes. It is a fit. It begins like this. The sentences are formed in the mind, but they come out as nonsense, or totally uncertainly. The rhythm is delivered, but the words, the phonemes, are chaotic, or simply the articulation stalls entirely. But then the sentence, after a moment, plays back in the mind, in the mind's ear, as if perfectly 'correctly'. I later learn this fore-signal is called an aura, and that what I am experiencing is a form of epilepsy, a small 'focal' fit, affecting a speech centre. And then I can't speak.

Or sometimes, I can't say the words I want to, though the words seem to be there to say. Likewise, I can't read aloud the words – or, in trying to read the words, the stress is completely cocked up. Whereas when I'm saying my own words the stress is the only thing I can manage. And can I understand written words when I read them silently? I'm not sure. It seems somehow possible. And then the fit ends, and I speak quite normally.

I have a rich variety of muddlings and loss. I can't always summon up names and proper nouns. I get crossed with opposite words (ask/answer, asleep/awake) or the right beginning of a word swaps with a wrong end. I switch around phonemes within phrases and sentences. I make Spoonerisms and Malapropisms. On driving through Hackney, I say 'police steakhouse' instead of 'police stake-out'. I use wrong parts of speech, like gender, tense, number. I find that I can't deliver poetry in a proper rhythm.

Therefore the problem is mainly in idiomatic, clichéd, everyday talk. And the speech that requires more attentive or inventive language comes out right. One is more aware of what one says. The speech that goes wrong is the speech that should actually deliver itself quite correctly, automatically, unthinkingly. It was already there to be said. And the fact that it goes wrong makes it clear that its normally reliable mechanism has failed. Unless I really slow down and pay attention, it will go wrong quite often. Yet I am still managing to write and to communicate clearly much of the time.

Further things. After the operation there are failures of casual hearing. I can only hear what I specifically pay attention to. I have difficulty obtaining a general overview of my mental field. I have a narrow, tunnel vision.

My writing becomes more fluent and fast.

Diagnosis

8 October 2008

Remember: stay open to weakness. Be open to fear and humiliation and dependency. Be open to helplessness and help. Be prepared for the story to be long and indefinite. (I realise I want the story to be done now, over – knowing that's very unlikely.) Understand yourself as not fully an agent; in a struggle, but not a struggler, but (mainly) a passive element in a struggle process, though hoping I have some strength. The body goes wrong; it can also be repaired.

Before: after. Before the diagnosis, we're eating in a restaurant nearby. I'm making notes. For the first time I've had before me a range of possibilities, from much better to much worse, waiting for it, not knowing what, counting down the time. In the circumstances it's unavoidable that hope will find a way under my guard.

Previously, the main result arrived all at once, and much sooner than I expected, and on the phone: there it was, a tumour, probably malignant. The news came before I was waiting for it. Now we have a day, a time, a meeting approaching. Gnawing hope.

And now I can't help imagining getting the better news – and then looking back upon my previous (i.e. present) fears and shrugging them off – and then feeling a kind of 'survival guilt' towards my past, meaning this present state of fear, as if I shouldn't abjure it – but knowing I'll be unable to resist skipping away from that past. In other words, there is, at this moment, only one kind of future I can bear to look at – a relatively good result – and other futures I keep my eyes away from.

Waiting. I have the metal pins that hold my wound together removed.

The meeting. Mr Kitchen. We are all very calm. The results are, in the circumstances, as bad as they can be. The most active level of malignancy. Very quick-growing. It is hard to estimate, but it has not been in my head for longer than a year, perhaps less time. Six weeks of radiotherapy and some pills. Basically, there is no plan B. And even if I survive, I can expect the cancer to return at some point. It's good they caught it so soon and small. Good they removed it so successfully, everything they could see of it. But it can be assumed that some traces remain. We don't say, but evidently, or so it strikes me, if the treatment fails, I will be dead within a year roughly.

Before, after. The present wipes out the preceding. What before was possible, and kept from clear sight, is now absolute, irrevocable. And the other possibilities are out of sight. It's impossible to honour the feelings of the immediate past. If it had been good news, the fears of bad would have been cancelled. Bad news, so no way to hold on to the hopes of good news. There is now only this situation, and the possibilities that issue from that. The flow chart has come to this point, and has only this branch now, and the rest is cut off, stemmed. It still has forks and ramifications ahead. But at some point along the way, there are no further forks. The chart will go on in one line only.

Imagining futures. Not much, in fact, imagining of the radiotherapy as such, and whatever grief that will give me. I'm thinking of further futures. One future: I survive, for a time anyway, and I look back upon this ordeal. (Again, imagining a future in which I look back upon the bad past, as something I've got through.) Another future: the treatment fails, and I face – more quickly or slowly – the approaching of my end, and the attendant dissolution of me. (And not looking back from that future.) What different futures!

So another threshold waits, another forking of paths, at some point, not so far ahead, another lot of tests and waiting for results, when I will hear whether the treatment has worked or not worked. Before: after. And I try to imagine waiting for that. I try to imagine how I will conduct myself, going towards dying.

Facing leaving Marion and Eugene, our growing old together, E's growing up. But not (as I now feel) for myself needing much more length of life. I know all the happiness and love I've felt I could know. My mind's work has basically done what it can do. Love and work can of course be extended indefinitely, but, give or take, I don't feel uncompleted, having missed out. I don't feel an *if only* hanging over me, out of reach. I've found what I could have found. Extinction in itself is not my grief.

(But if I die of this tumour, I will not face an abrupt ending, I will probably enter gradually into worsening degrees of incapacity. Of course I would want to die more quickly. Thoughts about suicide possibilities.)

I am expecting that I will die quite soon. I'm not expecting to survive. And to be sure, when the forking of paths approaches, I will find that I cannot remotely imagine it, and can only imagine a future of life. And when I find, all the same, that I'm on the dying line – well, what then? At the moment, in one frame of mind, it is incredible. In another, it must be.

*

It's not quite true to say that the past feels irrevocable. There is disappointment.

You do imagine back to one good possible (not so serious danger), and then imagine the other good possible (successful treatment).

You can't but imagine back as well, to the point where better outcomes were still possible.

I'm unable to prevent the mind shuttling forward (and to an extent backward too); trying to imagine what one will feel in future circumstances (or looking back to one's past anticipations). This is an endemic condition.

Teaching dying

Bertolt Brecht observed: 'Although the purely biological death of the individual is of no interest to society, dying ought nevertheless to be taught.'

William Empson on Tennyson's 'Tithonus': 'It's a poem in favour of the human practice of dying . . .' It is the phrase 'human practice' that holds the mind; its double surprise.

Human, as opposed to? Angels, divinities (because immortal)? Or animals (because, though mortal, not conscious of their mortality)?

And practice? – when it would be more normal to say 'condition' or 'fate' – and said as if we knew well what that practice was. Well, there are ways in which dying is a practice, among other rites of passage; and we can imagine it also as a rite of non-passage, as a conclusion. I'm trying to be in favour of the human *practice* of dying. Trying to make it into a practice.

No fingers crossed.

No probabilities. Only possibilities – or (so far as possible) certainties.

Without pessimism or optimism.

Holding your allegiance to the world, even while accepting your links to it are very weak.

About perspectives: people say, 'It puts things in perspective'. But for me, I need other things to put it in perspective. I need to hold several perspectives together.

Yet there is a transcendent aspect: living without the future, without an imagined future. There are moods when you feel you know something that not every one knows. But you also realise that this knowledge is growing – as it approaches, it gets better. You think at one stage you know something; but then later you find you know it better. And now, better yet by far.

Grief: you don't miss the present, when you aren't there to experience it. You do miss the future, when you know you won't be there to be experience it. So much of our joy of life lies in imagination. This is not an illusion, either. Or, you miss a-present-with-a-future.

(And you do miss the past, when you could still entertain that imagination.)

I'd imagined that I might need to take a few months off in convalescence. I imagined a caesura, another life afterwards, renewal. I didn't, now it seems, at first truly believe I might die, though I talked about it. And in fact it is a mystery, to be sure, to judge from now, what you do believe at various past points. But *now* I think, in about two months, or a few anyway, I will know whether I'm going to live or die – whether the treatment will have worked – however long after that I then live, and however long I keep my language and my wits.

This proved not to be how it proceeded.

Fear: to go into the radiotherapy, to be basically done by it, not to be cured by it, and lose language, and become terminally tired, and never to recover from it, to decline towards death, never saying goodbye properly, worst of both worlds.

Teaching being dead

In *Laughter* Henri Bergson gives the definition of comedy as the triumph of dead matter over living spirit. A man falls over in the street. A person is a slave to their bodily needs. A character is fixed in a repetitive psychological pattern.

These are basic comic situations. We laugh whenever human behaviour is rigid, compulsive, automatic. 'We laugh every time a person gives the impression of being a thing.'

In *The Act of Creation* Arthur Koestler replies: 'If we laugh each time a person gives the impression of being a thing, there would be nothing more funny than a corpse.' A good knockdown answer, but it's not quite the last word. *Corpses are funny*. At least, they're good material for comedy. A cadaver on stage or screen is often a comic turn. It's something that's got to be concealed. It must be lugged about with great difficulty. It has to be temporarily passed off as a living body. It won't stay properly dead, it keeps falling into lifelike postures and gestures.

Corpse-comedy: the basic joke goes two ways. Sometimes a corpse is like an extremely obstinate, uncooperative and insensitive person, who refuses to make any effort or response. And sometimes a corpse is like a weirdly animated object, a thing that can't help showing signs of life, involuntarily embracing or bashing or leaning affectionately on some other party.

A cadaver is like a person who gives the impression of being a thing – or, conversely, like a thing that gives the impression of being a person. At least, that's where the comic potential of corpses lies. It doesn't mean that a corpse is always comic. It only means that a corpse is an inherently troubling entity, an unstable hybrid of a person and a thing.

Comedy is one way of bringing this trouble out, not the only way. But when I imagine myself as a corpse ...

10 October 2008

At home. A quite serious fit; loss of speech; disorientation; limbs lose control; get myself to bed.

17 October 2008

After another meeting, with Lucy Brazil, the oncologist in St Thomas's, who I used to know slightly. I'm not especially expecting 'news', but news does, it seems, emerge. Though no figures or probabilities are explicitly stated, it leaves me the impression that, having perhaps been kept at bay by the treatment, the cancer might well return quite swiftly afterwards. Or rather, the most specific dating is this: I'm looking through a printout of possible side effects of radiotherapy. One is cancer. I point out that she hasn't mentioned it. She says: that would happen in perhaps ten years time, and you won't live that long. Then there are averages. I come away thinking I have about 2 years, perhaps, to live.

My death is imminent, now. I now say to myself: I am dying. Something in my head is hurrying to kill me.

19 October 2008

I write this email to Jeremy, but don't send it.

'I saw my oncologist on Friday morning. Did I mention that she – Lucy Brazil – is somebody I used to know, about 12 years ago? She was the flatmate of a friend. She's a very nice woman, a strange stroke of luck in the circumstances. Still, the meeting was one of those hole-and-corner affairs – the important ones always seem to go like that: office with two doors, somebody else barges in in the middle, obviously under pressure of time; not that it seems to matter, sensitivity is hardly the issue. Immediately afterwards I was fitted with my head mould, and the fitter was himself a total fuss, a comedy turn – just couldn't get down to the job, kept going off on this irrelevant story or another, however much we tried to urge him to proceed (actually I think now he may have been waiting for the water to warm up to soften the mask).

'Lucy says that my affliction is very rare: a GP might expect to see it once in their career. But nor, given its aggressiveness, should I ever expect to escape it. It is only a question of deferring its return. Considering that my situation is relatively favourable though (tumour detected early and small, me youngish, goodish health) they will give me the maximum treatment, believing I will benefit. That is: six weeks of radiotherapy, plus an oral chemo pill at the same time (supposed not to make me feel like complete shit), and then the pill continued at a lower dose for the next six months. Still, as I say, there is not a question of getting out the other side of it. We haven't talked about times and probabilities, but my general understanding is that I will die in a few years' time; two years, say. Of course it may be longer or shorter – it is all unpredictable at the moment, as also is how much time will be lost to treatment and dying itself. But in another sense I consider myself to be dying now, a subject on which I have various thoughts. As for Marion and Eugene, and all the future we won't have, it is utterly heartbreaking. As for me, I wouldn't use the word "nightmare". I now have a clear sense of being something limited, and in that respect, it makes me feel quite real – albeit, to be deprived of that vague fringe of hopefulness, the sense of indefinitely open-ended imaginable prospect, which borders the living consciousness at all times, feels unnatural. I am both standing outside my life, in a rather transcendental state, and also more intensely within it.'

I hold on to the word 'fact'. I have something clear and solid about myself. I feel realer. Wittgenstein said 'good' when he was told for certain of his coming dying.

Here I am alive. At some point, not so long from now, I won't be.

You can die suddenly in mid-life.

Or you can be told it's on its way. One year. Two years.

Full stopping. All our imaginings of endings are in terms of continuings beyond that. Whatever is going on and will end, you suppose you'll be somehow looking back on what ended, from somewhere; and while it lasts you're always making provision for that self that will be continuing after, and whatever is now is for the sake of what comes after – *for the sake of what comes after* – always for the sake of what comes after; but in this case you will not be there; so it isn't (in that sense) for you; or if it is for you, it is for you for now, for the duration, not for later. Well, true, there are various posthumous aspects to your existence, but these shouldn't distract you from your full stopping. This is one lesson I try to teach myself, a lesson in imagination, in self-imagination: you will stop.

I feel absolutely this thing, this limited thing, that I am – and also, in apprising that, outside of myself.

Again. I understand now that this is not something I'm going to get through or over. The coming on will only be deferred. ('In remission': which biologically I don't understand, in fact.) I had understood this before, after the biopsy report. Do I now understand it more clearly? Because the odds, the lengths, seem reduced?

There is a privilege in this position. Seeing your limitation. Seeing yourself as a thing in the world. Seeing the world as something continuing outside and beyond yourself. Though of course you aren't confronted, except in imagination, with your own vanishing, with your own transition from living body to corpse.

The rest of the world exists: affirm that.

All our language of dying seems to imply continuing in some form – we put it as leaving, returning, sleeping – there's something that still goes on.

I had probably misjudged my future – seeing it as a choice between either getting past the present crisis, or going on straight away to the end. It now looks more like going on, but not for very long; but for how long?

To die in itself, is nothing. Stop.

I feel the need to disburden myself of my bad news, of my destruction.

It will be a few years only, and those few years will not be a time of life, and then end, but a continual struggle to stay alive, followed by a dying process.

What I lose now, most generally, is the indefinite, open-ended prospect of life; not any particular goals but all the unknown imaginable goods, which always fill the edge of your view. Our life is lived on those terms, of ongoingness. They are the assumption. Without them, our life appears alien.

Two problems of imagination: accepting that you will fully end. Accepting life without a long prospect.

Yes. These problems are everybody's mortality. But not too soon.

I'm cheering myself with the thought that I am now made certain. Before, I lived in all kinds of apprehensions about what might be wrong or right. Now they have all been concentrated into this, that is definitely and gravely wrong. A fatal diagnosis is a sovereign cure for hypochondria.

20 October 2008

Having said to friends at the weekend: *I am dying*, I had to correct it in an email:

'... but after what I said then, I should tell you that this evening Marion said to me: You do know that I fully intend to be with you for another ten years (she had seen how my thoughts were tending) and I could only answer: Yes, why the hell not! Of course, I can't help considering all my worst possibilities, but I've probably too quickly adopted the role of moribund. So, until further notice, I am alive.'

Talking to Jeremy. Why did Lucy emphasise that it was incredibly bad luck? That a tumour as aggressive as this is extremely rare, so you are very unlucky to have it. Was it meant to make me feel in some way better? He agreed that it was, and that there was a kind of reasonableness to this intention, though we couldn't quite say why. I could really feel sorry for myself? It was very unfair, unjust? I could feel that right was on my side? As if the gods or a personified universe had slipped into the transaction? But I may say that, of the various religious temptations – prayer for help, belief in survival after death – I haven't been visited by the feeling that some power is afflicting me.

Or was it simply as an apology for the universe: things can be that bad, but it's very uncommon.

21 October 2008

How long is long enough to become indefinite? How much time stops looking like a death sentence and starts looking like a vague fringe extent of life ahead?

Suppose I said: I can't stand it – what would I do? This is not a marriage I can leave, a job I can resign, a country I can emigrate from, a prison I can try to escape. There are no terms to be come to. I could kill myself, so as to escape the intolerability of dying. Almost imaginable. I could try to get myself into a state where nothing that makes it matter to me does matter. Then I would be, in effect, already dead.

I used to think that, faced with dying, you should (as it were) go into a monastery, turn away from life and turn wholly towards death; lie in one's coffin. I thought it was a mark of silliness, superficiality, evasiveness, deceivedness, to try and go on living as if your previous life counted. But now I don't think that. But it is true, at the stage that I am at, I don't understand how to maintain the various perspectives together. Teaching dying, if it could be done, would be in part to teach you how to keep your view on both life and death.

I used to think that it was wrong to say: our thoughts go out to the bereaved. No, our thoughts should go out first of all to the dead, to those who experienced gradual dying or sudden death, who – whatever they knew about it – had suffered the outrageous deprivation of life. But now I don't think that. The dead can take it.

The scandal of death? Better to have no death on earth? Better to have much longer lives? Better to have some more merciful transition between life and death? Better to keep open resurrection possibilities, in the far future, cryogenically? We can imagine all kinds of alternative arrangements.

Obviously my death will be untimely – untimely by the accident of my life situation, by the vigour still left in me. I should live on, with Marion, with Eugene, and to work. That is an argument for better medicine. I will be dying early of inadequate medicine. In the future, possibly people won't die of what I will.

I feel very open to happiness and sadness, but not to despair or depression. Today I am quite elated. Yesterday in the wind and cloudiness in the park, all sadness.

The afflicted have no exclusive insight in these matters.

As Tom Sutcliffe pointed out last night, variously:

I will get bored of talking about myself under this aspect.

This incredibly bad news has had an initial exhilarating, energising effect, which will wear off. And then what?

I don't have a dated death sentence.

I have several life expectations in common with most – to outlive the day, the week, the month, the six months, the year, perhaps ...

... and it seems that any margin of indefinite future is enough to count as a prospect, as something.

I thought that his observations were fine, and that the well have a perfect right to make observations about the afflicted; and that many wouldn't have the nerve, but he was good that he did. The difference is that the afflicted are likely to go on at the subject more continuously, and not to feel that it's exhausted.

Normally we take no interest in the fact that someone died, and very little in how. But I'm presuming that I do know how I will die – and the fact that I'm going to die, the brevity of my expected life ahead, and how it modifies my experience, is the most interesting thing about me.

Today I am thinking and feeling so lightly, I'm not sure I really believe in my mortality. And at any time, whatever I may say, I can never be sure I really believe. I have a problem of faith. Or will there be a time when I feel the force of belief, through its terrible grip – or through the counter-force of my resistance to its terror?

I had been saying: no optimism. That it seems, applied to the question of news. But as to the length of my life with Marion and Eugene, there seems to be no question of anything but optimism. We must live together as long as we can. We must hope.

22 October 2008

Today I realise there is a spring in my step. It returns to me that I have been given something.

And this evening I glanced again through the research paper on my treatment, and meet again the fact that my life expectancy is indeed unlikely to be more than two or three years, and I feel downcast. And how much of that lost to dying? And through what decline?

23 October 2008

Someone who dies at 50+ is not thought to have had a bad life. You found out who you were, what you wanted, what you were up to. Not a long life, a short one, obviously, but not ruinously short. Not, of course, that someone else can't live for a double span.

25 October 2008

The living thing strives to live. The living thing has a stop.

That striving, that limitedness, can be expressed in the same shape; can be embodied in the same strength.

The shape of the will to live is also the shape of its limitedness.

What makes the figure so strongly living is the enclosure that contains it.

The shape of life and death are one.

That shape is where life and its end meet.

The limit is the counter-pressure or cut-off.

The shape of the creature is the pressure of life against the limit of death.

Reluctantly, I find myself feeling more mystical. The mind at times going dreamlike, as if going into a transitional state, to assure myself that the difference between life and death can be blurred; it occurs involuntarily, a heightened state, passive, opening, embracing, spreading, dispersing, feeling out, somewhat ecstatic; moving away by moving your attachments outwards, your coordinate points, breaking down your edges – not killing these attachments, but similar in general effect to stoicism, to make one not mind.

John K's friendly tactlessness puts me at my ease.

26 October 2008

Seeking the pre-emptive dissolution of the self ...

Likewise, I felt drawn into a church service on the radio this morning. Into either its ongoing timeless ritual, or its low-level supernaturalism; the self, drifting away, drifting off; half-asleep; rocking, dozing.

A new motto: neither mysticism nor stoicism.

But also: I'm drawn to apocalyptic feelings; the world is coming in for a destruction that will match my own.

This afternoon: at home, doing home chores, music on, Marion building shelves, Eugene playing by himself around our feet: perfect, beautiful calm, peace, happiness, patience, attention, acceptance. (Eugene – he is me!)

Patience. The end that will come too soon. The knowledge that must be waited for.

It seems my spirit depends on strength, clarity, activity – and on the other hand, physical weakness and making a visit to hospital. I am putting death out of thought and letting it back in.

Treatment

3 November 2008

For the last week I have felt well, and clear and active in the head. I see I have not thought about my affliction or my death. I have lost the knack, it seems. I have moved away from that view. I fully disbelieve in my troubles and prospects. I feel as if I have unlimited life. I'm as of old. The preceding mortal perspectives have no hold on me. But I know I will be back with them at some point. I ought to keep them in my sights all the time – along with other perspectives. If only to encourage me to do what's needed to prolong my life.

All I have in anxiety at the moment is the beginning of my therapies tomorrow.

About radiotherapy.
My drivers:
Mondays: Jeremy Canty

Tuesdays: Vivien Ashley
Wednesdays: Cab service, provided by Victoria Miro
Thursdays: Laura Cumming
Fridays: Mark Wallinger

I enjoy the firm clamping down of the head. Not particularly that I appreciate or suppose that it's doing me good. I like the feeling of it, being manipulated and held.

No ill effects yet.

11 November 2008

To Jenny Polak, email:

'In fact, I'm feeling well. No side effects have appeared yet from either side of the treatment. The experience of being head-clamped to the radiotherapy table – you have a closely moulded mask, like a wide mesh fencing mask, fixed down hard – is surprisingly nice, a solid feeling, as the table rotates and levitates and the machines orbit and buzz. You can bring your own CDs. Bach keyboard so far. Of course things may get worse. At the moment I am confused by realising that for the last fortnight I have ceased to think of myself as a mortal, in the ways I was thinking before that. I just seem to be carrying on mentally as my old pre-mortal state.

'Anyway, I feel this is wrong, though it is also happy. I just find I cannot focus my mind at all on my previous objects. Not that it won't all return at some point. People say: it must put everything in perspective, or you see more clearly, or whatever, but just now it's not so at all. This feels like disbelief kicking in. Not what I want.'

13 November 2008

I have been worrying and training myself back into a mortal state. Calling myself a mortal. Noticing, as before, that to see oneself as a mortal is also to see oneself as, in a sense, an immortal – that is, one who has moved out of the normal round whose condition is not to see oneself as mortal.

Mortality + self-consciousness = immortality!

The surreal formula, making the extraordinary ordinary and the ordinary extraordinary: it is true for me now, too bad. The magic spell of cancer, once a word of fear and trembling and wonder, is now my daily talk. Blastoma.

17 November 2008

Laura sends me an email:

'Have you read an essay by Stephen Jay Gould called *The Median Isn't the Message*? I came across it last week, with much pleasure, and thought of you.'

I read it. I was struck, not so much by its measuredly encouraging message, as by this:

> It has become, in my view, a bit too trendy to regard the acceptance of death as something tantamount to intrinsic dignity. Of course I agree with the preacher of Ecclesiastes that there is a time to love and a time to die – and when my skein runs out I hope to face the end calmly and in my own way. For most situations, however, I prefer the more martial view that death is the ultimate enemy – and I find nothing reproachable in those who rage mightily against the dying of the light.

What struck me is that I may be susceptible to this trendiness. SJG calls it trendy, I suppose, mindful of Elisabeth Kübler-Ross's influence, and her stage-by-stage progression to the good end (denial, anger, bargaining, despair, acceptance) in which raging is to be surpassed and acceptance is to be sought.

It seems to me that my immediate response was: straight for acceptance! Fear of rejection!

18 November 2008

Dinner with Eric. He points out that three things have happened to me in the last few years that I might have expected never to happen to me. Getting married. Becoming a father.

Being diagnosed with a brain tumour. I assent, kind of.

He says: of course you don't ask 'why me', do you? I say: no, no, of course not.

Two possible whys there. Why, because there is some physical cause. There is no identified cause for such brain tumours, which are rare and random. Or why, because there is some metaphysical cause. As if the universe had it in for me.

19 November 2008

I think side effects are taking effect. Hairs are beginning to come out from the irradiated areas of my head. There is some muzziness in the mind. But I'm OK in the evenings.

'I must say, you're looking very well,' people say. So I am. But looks have nothing to do with it.

24 November 2008

I've fallen in love with Eugene.

27 January 2009

I've written no notes for two months. None really since the start of November, in which I've gone through the radio-therapy/ chemo combined treatments, without serious ill effects, and then – through Christmas and weeks subsequent – undergone some more stronger after-effects, of weakness, mental blurriness, speech slips, not speaking much, deep sleepiness and sleep (and some perhaps connected stomach upset). None of this is an encouragement to reflection; I'm simply getting through it, though it's not too bad, an ongoingness, a certain depression (not to mention Eugene's growing moodiness, and the pressure on Marion of my weakness and absent state).

But – thinking back to an earlier thinking forward – making the usual mental switch-back manoeuvre (it took me ages to spell that) – I remember fearing that the treatments would be the start of the end of everything. The brain would enter terminal fogging and never recover its clarity, and I would be thereafter in a (worsening) blur until the close of my life. This has not happened. Even though it has got worse since the treatments stopped, and I must anticipate future memory relapses, still I can continue my newspaper works and other writing, though no doubt that will be slower too. Next week I start doing reviews; long pieces, with opinions, needing to be written in a leisurely, spontaneous, conversational way.

Last week I started my new regime of chemo, at double dose, five successive days per lunar month, for six lunar months. I have not been in contact with the person in

California (a friend of a friend) who might be able to share their close experience in a useful way; and I hardly make any effort to find out facts about my condition or treatment, even though it becomes clear that medical people let them out in a very unsystematic way, so you discover things very randomly: recently I realised that the previous chemo course was designed in some way to make the malignancy more susceptible to the radio rays (I'd thought they were just two separate lines of attack). Lucy says: you are well, that is good news in itself, and I can see there is some sense in this, better than that I was clearly in a decline – but then I was well up to my fit.

Yesterday I had an MRI scan, the first diagnostic scan since just before the operation on 30 September. So this is, very nearly, four months on from the 'maximal debulking' surgery. I have been told that the scan may not show or tell much. The brain may not yet be readable, the tumour may seem to be growing whereas 'actually' it isn't ('pseudo-progression'): hold back from hope or fear; of course I do not. I expect to hear about the results in a couple of days. I anticipate results and my reactions to them. I have been thinking a bit in the last few weeks. I can't remember what. But to be sure, a more future-oriented perspective will open, one way or another.

Laura said someone might be interested in running something that I might write about all this. I said there is a narrative problem. I don't know at what stage, and in what story, I am. The normal condition of any life-telling, yes, at least in the long-term. But also at any time we live in stories, shapes, trajectories: we have envisageable ends, and envisageable paths towards them. Some conditions such as mine would be clearly moribund, and some would be looking to recovery, and some would be hoping for reasonable life prolongation, but I don't know what my narrative frame is – well, moribund, surely enough, but span is all.

I was getting to the age of beginning to envy those younger than me, for all the usual normal reasons, for having done already what I have not yet and probably now won't; but now I have begun to envy those older than me, simply for having lived longer than I will, for their sheer years.

19 February 2009

The scan revealed as expected very little, it seems, so I made no record of the results when I heard them a week later. There is some evidence of tumour. Or it was stable, as a registrar said? Or some 'rind', it was called in a later letter. What it's doing, what's going on, I've no idea.

Mortal: that is, death is more imminent than my age would normally promise, more likely than the normal chances of accidental death ...

'Why should a dog, a horse, a rat, have life, And thou no breath at all?'

And me? Evidently this is a natural wicked thought, and I do not normally harbour it – though I entertain it, about humans, not animals. I look at the loony man who sits on the wall at the end of the street, and I think: well, surely the world is better off with me than him. Though at other times I think, if offered the chance of swapping fatality with someone else, and doing it without it ever being known, and no Faustian pay-off – simply the devil says: she/he dies young, you get to live on, and you get away with it, but be clear, you do choose her/his early death – I would not choose this other's death. But why? Since, from an objective view, it is equal between one untimely death and another, why shouldn't it be not mine? Because I mustn't be selfish? From a respect for fact, as if fact was fate? Or suppose the devil makes a different offer. I swap my chances of longevity with another, not knowing the odds. Their life might prove shorter than mine.

24 March 2009

I should ask: when the course of chemo is over, what then? I guess they scan, they see what's going on. And if they find something they don't like the look of?

And at some point I must ask:

1 How will I know that my dying has begun? (Will I know clearly?)
2 What form will it take? Pain? Deficits? Delusions? Derangements? Incapacitation? Unconsciousness? And for how long?

Three annoying sympathisers:

1 Those who come only wanting to have their minds put at rest.
2 Those who know someone who had exactly what you've got, and she's absolutely fine now.
3 Those who want you to know they realise just how awful it is for you – and with the little one!

Afterlife: Julian Barnes believes that if he believed in a God, he would believe in an afterlife. And he believes that if he believed in an afterlife, he would want to go there too. But many modern believers are not so sure about there being an afterlife. And many ancient believers were terrified of it. So he wants the best of both ages. He wants, like an ancient, to be sure that there will be an afterlife; and, like a modern, to be sure that, if there is one, it will be welcome.

26 May 2009

The weeks pass so quickly between chemo weeks. Eugene, and my slightly slower rate of work, and slight fatigue, fill everything. We move from weekend to weekend. M & I hardly have any time to loll around. And for many, many weeks I haven't thought of doom, and am obviously disbelieving in it, feeling more and more that I will survive almost indefinitely, or at least not finitely enough to think about it. I am feeling better, since the start of the year. The side effects are wearing off.

A few days ago I sent this email to Lucy:

'I think we're due to meet on Fri 5 June, before my last week of chemo.

'Obviously that raises the question: and what after that?

'At some point then I will have another scan. I don't know whether that can be expected to produce a clear result, one way or the other. But I feel that we should have a conversation about possible futures before those futures loom into view, and with their possible fears becoming too present. And I wonder if we could have a meeting before the scan, that was outside the time pressure of your hospital appointment schedule, to talk about these things.

'I have now got my steroids down to 1mg a day again. I have had no repetition of the relapse the other day. I am generally feeling well.'

Marion's tears from time to time. We don't speak. We assume what it means – my dying, my death, my not being here, our losses, hers, mine, Eugene's, whenever it happens, what we have to say to him, how it goes. I don't cry, or hardly ever. I try to look at it hard. As if my dry eyes were my strength.

Tears: but there are so many causes for tears; the fact that we have this particular cause for tears need not impress us. Is it the worst? I have been unhappier, no? Situations. Getting bad news. Waiting for bad news. Compare now with other fears, blows. In childhood, in youth. My heart has beaten harder.

4 May 2009

Small fit. While talking to Dan on the phone.

10 May 2009

Small fit. While out with Marion, at Tate Modern.

7 June 2009

Small fit. While Marion is in Hastings. Long sleep.
   Marion and I walk and talk.

17 June 2009

We had a meeting with Lucy. We talked about epilepsy as a side effect, and auras. We talk about further possibilities of treatment. 800mg Epilim.

Good News

9 July 2009

First MRI scan for six months.

16 July 2009

On the phone from Lucy: 'Very good news' from scan.

21 July 2009

Neurologist. 1,000 mg Epilim.

25 July 2009

Very small fit. Marion out buying a paddling pool. Eugene asleep. Tim comes round, Marion comes back miraculously by hailing a passing, already occupied taxi in south London.

14 August 2009

Very small fit while on the cross-London train, starting off for France.

23 August 2009

Very small fit. After Jane and Jiri's visit. While preparing chicken stock.

22 October 2009

Tomorrow I see Lucy and will perhaps get results from yesterday's MRI scan.

Last time's were very good. But that was just after the six months of chemo. This time, after three months of no treatment? I don't think about death. (Nor about dying.)

I will die first. Then Marion. Then Eugene. (We hope so. Any other order would be catastrophic for me, or for Marion, or for us. Eugene as a survivor would, I assume, manage the death of either and both parents.) But my thought is: eventually, one by one, the world will be cleared of us, and I picture it as earth, not the earth one might be buried in, but the surface on which we are now standing: that is how I picture death – not as some force that ploughs us down, but as a solid mass, the ground that remains after us, and on which we once lived and from which we drew our life. Perhaps the earth will be cleared of all mankind one day. (Everyone dies; some die without issue; suppose everyone died so.) The earth, immovable, our supporter and survivor.

What to tell Eugene, when we tell him that I will die? That I won't be here. My body will stop. Sleeping and more than sleeping, never waking, never moving, never speaking. And after – that we don't know? I'd be prepared to say that, if I still had the power of speech. But truly I don't believe it. I'm not an agnostic about the afterlife. I don't believe there is something that is me that could be elsewhere from my body – and my body is evidently taken care of.

This view is complicated by various things. Mental activity can continue with very restricted bodily powers. You can have a mind without facial expression, without gestures, or without voice or tone of voice, without sensation. (Stephen Hawking, *The Diving Bell and the Butterfly*). The soul may return after a long comatose absence (*Awakenings*). Mental activity, in a quite normal way, proceeds without apparent bodily signs: lost deep in thought. So we may think soul, or mind, is separable from body. Helen Waddell gazing into senile vacancy for years: her biographer wonders what marvellous visions she was granted! I'm imagining that that may happen to me.

Limits: you feel all that you're losing (anything that catches your eye), but equally, the fact that you're losing it makes you conscious that it itself is a limited thing: languages, customs, beauties, societies, cultures, historical periods, anatomies, species, continents – everything began, will end, might be otherwise. You feel (in other words) like a radical alien, a visitor to the world. You see it in all its contingency, historicity, limitedness. (People say nature doesn't have history: of course it does, it has evolutions and revolutions, though generally slower than human ones.) We live in a world that is not infinite in any way. You can stand back, look down, see it in every aspect as something contained, provisional, provincial. Sub specie aeternitatis. Troilus in seventh Heaven. This is a kind of immortality – or at least super-mortality.

Death: my body stopped; or the earth, with me gone; or me, looking down on the world.

23 October 2009

The results are good again.

But this time I don't feel so elated by the good news. Of course bad news would be worse. But this good news makes me aware of this existence which will never end.

And I live in leases of three months: the distance between each scan.

I think this way: now I have another three months of clear life. Whatever goes well or ill with me over that time, it won't become fact until I get the result of the next scan. Whatever happens in my brain, won't come into existence until I'm told about it. The fact is the news. Or to break it down further: there's my brain; there's the scan; there's the doctors' reading of the scan; there's me being informed. And if I'm OK now, I'm OK until the very moment when I'm told I'm still OK/not OK, and (implied) I'll stay well until my next scheduled scan. Of course it may not work out that way, but that's how I think.

To put it more simply: as I imagine it, the good news will last for the next three months.

What name should I give to my state? Mortal? But we're all mortal, all the time. Terminal? But that implies an end too imminent. This thing that I have, unless I'm very unlucky or very lucky, is what will kill me. I mean, it will kill me quite soon. How many few years are left to me I don't know, but I cannot expect a long life. Fatal?

2 December 2009

There is only one universe. If there weren't, I could hope to go and live in another where the laws or the history were different. But in this one I live and I die.

What I mean is: I have bumped up against one of the laws of the universe; life dies; no exceptions.

Everything else has alternatives, or potential alternatives. If you're alive, you sooner or later die. Once you're dead, you're dead, there's no coming back, or going on, or being anything else.

Among all the believable things, this is the unbelievable thing.

I feel sad at this moment. I think of the reasons I have for being sad. But I notice that it feels like a sadness that I have felt, at moments, throughout my whole life. What was it, is it, sadness for? For something that once was, impossible to remember.

14 January 2010

Tomorrow I will hear the result of my most recent scan. I can't gauge the level of my fear – or of optimism, or pessimism.

'The readiness is all.' Oh, but for goodness' sake!

It is exhausting to live in these lots, terms, shifts, stretches, each coming to its three-monthly crisis, which one day will bring bad news.

Or rather, that was what I was meaning to write; but before I could, Marion took a call on her mobile, or rather missed it, took the message left on it, said 'good', put it to replay, passed it to me: Lucy saying she had had the chance to look at my scan and it was 'good'. This at 8 p.m. (She's never managed to get my own number.)

My first reaction: completely turned around, all my mental preparation for tomorrow is suddenly thrown out ahead of time. How glad I am. How afraid I had been that my luck would have run out. But then it calms into a sense that this is as it should be, of course I should have a normal life, a life I can take for granted. And then it turns to resentment that there should be any question of this, that the question comes up as it does, every three months.

The word 'good' has become a magic word, meaning life itself.

26 January 2010

My story doesn't make a good story. A good story would either be a steady descent towards death, or a total recovery. But I have had, probably will have, a fluctuating plotline, with ups and downs, recoveries, declines, rallies, with some kind of final wreckage or fade. And so far I have seemed and felt pretty well all through. This is not an easy story for others to follow. For us, much of the time, it has been nail-biting.

I meet someone who thinks I am now better. I explain that the treatment went well, but in fact I will never be better. Sooner or later I will get worse, and then even worse. It's very strange having to live in these spans, waiting at some point for the bad news to come. She says: I suppose you have to live in the present. I say that it is actually not a very encouraging thought. And I'd recently seen a show – scientific-ish – which includes an exhibit about someone who really did live literally in the present. I tried to put it in a nice way.

What I had written in a review was that we should:

'pay a moment's attention to the experience of Clive Wearing. A moment is all he ever knows.

'A musician, who worked for the BBC, Wearing got a virus that struck his brain, giving him a rare form of amnesia. His handwritten diary is one of the most extraordinary bits of text I've seen for quite a while. Here is part of the entry for April 21 1990.

11.06 a.m. Now I am nearly completely awake.
11.30 a.m. I return just as I am almost perfectly awake.
11.34 a.m. First, almost totally conscious stroll. I am perfectly awake.
12.39 p.m. Now I am almost really perfectly awake.
1.20 p.m. Now I am almost actually completely awake.

'And it's weird that all these *nearly*s and *almost*s are inserted into the sentences like qualifying afterthoughts. But so he goes on.

3.26 p.m. Now I am nearly perfectly awake.
3.51 p.m. Now I am nearly completely awake.
4.09 p.m. Now I am nearly totally awake.
4.20 p.m. Now I am nearly overwhelmingly awake.
5.19 p.m. Now I am nearly superlatively awake ...

'Next time someone tells you that we should all try to live in the present, you'll know what they mean.'

And of course, even with a longer view, as I have, the loss of a proper prospect is precisely what you miss – the 'one day', the open future, the possibility of relaxation that gives to life. This constant constraint of brevity: either you have to forget about it, or you observe it as an extreme discipline. Not for me, that.

25 March 2010

I have thought up a misleading syllogism, whose misleadingness enlightens. It goes like this. I find the world is good; therefore I want to be in the world; therefore also the world is good without me.

That sounds good. It's a spell against mortality. The point is: we have a totally impersonal delight in life. The available quantity of the world's good continues, with or without my enjoyment of it, and is hardly altered by the presence of this or that particular person – e.g. me. (After all, anyone's personal contribution to the world, in terms of love or work, however large, is still relatively small.)

But this syllogism is also deceitful. I don't enjoy the world as something separate to me. I and the world are mixed up together. What I enjoy about the world is partly but inextricably my enjoyment of it *by myself*. The good of the world I experience is the world *as* experienced by me. And so the loss of me to the world, as far as I am concerned, is a serious loss to me too. I can't imagine the world's good as apart from my perspective.

So, the world's good, life's good, has an objective and a subjective aspect. In one way I can cheer the world, whether I'm there or not. In the other way, the world only exists as I know it, and will cease to exist when I cease to exist; this won't matter much to anyone else, to me it matters absolutely.

Or briefly: I want life in the world because the world is good. But the world is good without me too. And if my contribution to the world's good is little, I could contemplate my absence with equanimity. But I cannot see the world as equally good with or without me – simply because without me, there won't be the particular way in which only I can enjoy it. The good of the world includes my unique way of experiencing it, and for me that is almost all.

My speech is now becoming a radical problem.

Sometimes, for a short period, and suddenly, I find that I no longer know what I am saying, but I still go on talking, and talking sense – like an inspired sibyl or a medium. The voice works automatically, fluently, subconsciously, through habit or practice. The words would need to be looked up, if I could recognise their spelling. But I can recognise at least that my speaking is correct, and I am aware that my words and phrases are familiar and appropriate ...

(By the way: my typing here encounters all sorts of glitches, sometimes pointed up by spell-check and grammar-check – thank goodness – sometimes by my own sense of rightness. A moment ago, trying to write 'at least', I was strongly inclined to write 'itself', phrases that share t, l, s. I could give countless examples. And thank goodness, also, that my texts are not covered all over by manuscript rewrites.)

... and likewise, I can hear others' words, and accept them as meaningful and familiar, without being able to repeat or paraphrase or interpret their meaning, though I can perhaps reply sensibly, or at least act sensibly in reply. At a particular subconscious level, speech is functioning. Consciously, I can't spell some words, I don't know what they mean, I can't recite their phonemes. All I can recognise is the phatic role of my words, their tone.

To put this another way. One can have quite extended conversations more or less on autopilot. Not brilliant, but perfectly functional. (Such as making a basic transaction in a shop.) But most other people, if you then ask: 'what did you say just now?' would be able to recap their words – repeating, rephrasing, explaining. I couldn't do this at all. My speech comes from somewhere, obviously, but it doesn't reach my surface understanding. Likewise with words spoken on the radio. It all makes sense until you ask, and then it's all blank.

Something else. For a period, suddenly, I cannot speak (or read aloud) any words, except the most short, simple, basic. They are fine. And all the rest, the more complex words, come out as a kind of garbled gobbledegook. Yet the stress of all the words and sentences – sense or nonsense – is equally and perfectly accurate. I know what I mean to say, and to a hearer what I say moves fluently, though in and out of meaningfulness. The simple and comprehensible words punctuate a sequence vocalised out of nonsense.

Generally, I know what I'm saying – and likewise I can understand what is spoken to me and what I read, though I can't repeat those words. My ability to write is variable, but generally greater. I have different capacities in different registers.

Let me try to differentiate these activities (and failures in them):

Speaking my own words – finding the words at all, articulating them properly, finding them familiar, consciously understanding them.

Hearing another's words – recognising them at all, finding them familiar, consciously understanding them, being able to repeat them, holding on to information in a list.

Reading aloud a text – articulately, understandingly.

Reading a text silently – understanding it.

Writing my own text – finding words, putting them down correctly, fluently, articulately, like speech.

Copying another text – correctly.

The point is: they do not fail at the same time, to the same degree.

Finding the words.

It is a permanent mystery how we summon up a word. Where are these connections located in the mind? How do we know how we do it, and get it right? This mystery becomes – 'becomes', not 'because', please – evident when our ability to summon up our words fails.

We assume that all the different registers of language that we use – and of course there are several registers – are happily parallel operations. Well, they are separate. But at the same time, they interact and reciprocally correct themselves. For example: I can often lose one register of language, but not another. I might lose my understanding of words' spelling and the composition of their phonemes. I become spelling-blind and phoneme-deaf. Meanwhile my fluent, unselfconscious speaking is more or less unimpaired.

Now suppose that my speaking also encounters a small snag. Normally I could assist myself by calling up, by envisaging, the letters or the phonemes of the words, and spelling out more carefully and consciously the pronunciation. Now I can't. And I become aware of this. I try, but I cannot visualise a letter.

Illiterates would never be able to do this. Their speech would never be assisted by this knowledge. The conclusion is that speaking and reading are not distinct capacities. Nor is writing simply an add-on, nor is it merely a matter of letters; it involves sound recognition and naming. The literate speaking is different from the illiterate speaking.

Another level of ability. My speech gets snagged. I know what the word is, but I can't pronounce it rightly – the vowels go wrong, or the consonants, or the number of syllables, or quite often the stress. How do I correct the failure? Sometimes the resources of literacy won't help. But relaxing, letting go of my self-consciousness, going by instinct, will. Let it run.

Equally, I might remember another context in which the word occurs. It can be drawn from many different dockets. I couldn't say for example: Mr Deputy Speaker; I could only say Depéwter, Depéwter – until I recalled

Deputy Dawg, which gave me the right inflection, and the vowel followed too.

So I speak (and read aloud) reasonably well, but come out with a lot of errors in articulation, requiring several attempts. Once I have practised a word, or been told what it is, it comes all right. The way forward may be strenuous, or it may be through relaxation, but with practice it comes; and then I've got it.

Again, tomorrow, the span of scan is up. No idea: hope, fear. Some surprising fits recently, and my expectation always of luck running out, arouse fears of bad news; but there is no clear evidence – whatever clear evidence would be.

Sometimes I feel that I am not quite well now, in relation to language, and then I want to know what is wrong; sometimes I feel I'm fine, and I want the results to be fine as before. I am as usual becoming fearful.

Last time, Lucy rang ahead, bringing good news. At that time, I said that if you were to bring bad news, you wouldn't ring, you would tell me face to face. So no call ahead of the appointment will probably be a sign of bad news. So next time, so I don't have any expectation either way, please don't necessarily ring me if the news is good. Let no call mean nothing. Well, there has been no call. She may have remembered my request, leaving the question open. Or she may have forgotten it, and the news is bad, and she is doing what she would normally do in those circumstances. (Or she might be away, in which case I would be dealing with another doctor, who wouldn't be ringing me either way.)

Bad News

26 March 2010

Well, I don't know which it was, but the news is bad, and Lucy gave it to us face to face. There are signs of activity in the tumour. My recent increased speech glitches – words escaping me, mispronunciations – indicated this, and the scan showed it. Another course of treatment is due. Conceivably another operation, which I am very against, unless it is very safe or very badly needed. I'll have various kinds of chemo. Some more research is required. But in short: I'm back in the mortality business.

This bad news feels so irrelevant – it has nothing to do with what I want to do. But again, my life feels very irrelevant. So I myself am on hold between sickness and life.

How long did I want to live, given that my life was now abbreviated? How many scan-spans did I expect to go on, before the news turned bad? Three months more? Six months more? At some point this change would happen. And then what is now happening, would happen. Is the evil diminished by being deferred? Surely it is. We compose these mad consolations. You might as well say: one second of life is as good as a century. Die any time, and you might as well die now. But actually, life is length of life, nothing else, until life becomes intolerable.

Good news, continued, made me lazy. Now I am quickened.

I would like to get through the first shock and all its resonances, and get on with my attention.

What would it be like? I wondered. Now I know. The next step. I knew it would arrive at some point. There was no chance that it would be deferred for ever or for long. I wanted to know what this thing would be, this thing that I knew would come.

And the situation is absurd, absolutely absurd. A dying man – it's just not me! When he heard of my very first diagnosis, David Sexton wrote me: 'You had always seemed somehow an indestructible to me.' (Odd 'an'.) And I agree, in a way. I have felt as if I had in me a comic spirit of immortality. Nothing serious could touch me. Everything transcended. I'm not made for gloom. Not cast for catastrophe. I'm a riser-above, a floater.

But on the other hand, clowns are also those who display

their limitations, the body, its pratfalls, incompetence, falls, built-in failures; and cancer is above all a body-failure, a going-wrong, added on to all the others, and also on to the basic, built-in failure of mortality.

So mortality is a two-faced comedy. It is absurd to be mortal, bound to fall and fail. We should be able to do everything! But it is equally absurd to defy these limits, to rise above, to bounce back, to be invulnerable like a cartoon character, a real indestructible. For of course we aren't super-creatures, and these imaginings are against our nature, pure fantasy. (This fantasy is two-sided too: as a light floater and a thick rebounder, angel and blob.)

But we also have compound comic strength. We are blocks. We are solid, in double senses. We are stuck. We are immovable, inflexible. And we have a resistance, resilience. We have an intractableness.

There was that odd response I felt at the beginning, and which I articulated then as: 'What can harm me?' Meaning, partly I think, that because I now knew this worst, so I could stand outside myself as never before. But mainly meaning that recognising this destruction brooding within me made me feel real. I am a living and dying thing, a limited thing now, and no longer a bundle of indefinite possibilities. And 'Simply the thing I am shall make me live.' Stressing *the thing*.

27 March 2010

Perhaps for humans there is another case for being alive: from the perspective of the stadium. *The Year of Magical Thinking*. Joan Didion has lost a husband and shortly afterwards a daughter. She has lost 'everything'. She comes before us. Yet for all that, she, the survivor, has survived, and has the best of it, and can't but be seen as the winner; and her dead are the losers.

The Living: 1. The Dead: 0.

Imagine a cancer club, a terminals' support group. A is doing well, another good scan. Well done! B is showing a turn for the worse. Oh, bad luck! Gradually they die off. Novices join. Long-term survivors emerge who do not die off. They are admired and then resented. It might be more tactful for them to withdraw, and reclassify themselves again as the living. There are mutters. She was given the 'all clear' years ago, but she still turns up. What does she want? A prize?

28–30 March 2010

At the time, I had begun even to resent the good results, though of course being also immensely grateful; to have to live in these spans! But reading over the dates, looking back on that run of good results, now ended, I find I'm cheering them along. Good for my luck, keeping it up, for even such a short time.

Easter is coming. Christians on the radio. The resurrection is the defeat of death. But isn't that the ultimate blasphemy? Life is a thing with a beginning and an end. That's what makes life real.

('Death is the mother of beauty'? Not quite. Wallace Stevens's voice is too elegiac, a fade-out on repeat. A proper song should have a proper end, even if very abrupt or discordant.)

True, the Christian immortality story is complicated, and various; but what is worse, or better? Unending and uninterrupted life on earth would be weird – with ageing, without ageing? Repetition, with or without consciousness? Translating into a next world, incomprehensible glory, damnation? Or the grey depressed half-life of the classical underworld and the modern spiritualist realm? That seems the most convincing picture, if there must be an afterlife at all, the one that measures the ending of earthly life as pure loss.

The belief in immortality makes life on earth too light. It is made too easy to lose. We won't be losing it really. At least, we're asked to accept a never-ending afterlife as a substitute for this life – somehow an imaginable version of our earthly lives, continuing; and we greedily accept this offer, without looking so closely at it, since it seems to hold enough of what we want unappeasably now: our goods, our loves, ourselves, preserved.

And on the other hand the lost belief in immortality makes earthly life intolerably heavy. We can't bear to lose it. Once we had this promise of not losing it, of holding on to it for ever. Now we don't. But we haven't got rid of the dream of its possibility, and this makes the losing of our life into a real loss. We must be able to lose it, really lose it, since we will; and not regret ourselves so much. We must become lighter beings.

In short, we swap one consolation for another. Once we tried to say: we never really die. Now we try to say: we do, but it doesn't really matter. Nice one.

Suppose I should want there to be a god, not as a guarantee for my eternal life (I can die), but as someone to remember me, or to contemplate my life, every moment of it, for ever – and your life too, especially the times we're going through now. That's something god could do for us, a totally unselfish act by god.

This new bad news. In one way it is much worse than the previous bad news; it promises a treatment that will presumably be worse, and which presumably will be less likely to be effective, too, and our hopes diminish. In another way, we and our friends too are likely to take it less seriously; we've been through this already, this isn't the first shock for us or them, we're getting used to it, we know the ropes.

Suicide pacts. Or an imminent expectation of death, but collective. Doesn't the shared prospect of death allay its pain? The more we lose life together, the less it seems a loss. We who die are not being outlived by so many. Death is not a loss in itself, but a loss only in comparison with those who are not losing it. (The pain of death is that we die alone.) Or, let's say, in comparison with our contemporaries. Suppose everyone dies at the same set time, a fixed term and equal lifespan. It seems horrible, if it is set: who does the setting? But if somehow this was our nature, wouldn't it soften the blow?

In the past, when stoned, I've wondered what it would be like, to be stoned and also in a knowingly fatal state. I imagined it would be monstrous, to be off my head like that, not to be in my perfect senses. Partly it seemed like an irresponsible dulling of myself. Partly I was terrified at the thought of where my mind might run, into free fall. I don't get stoned now. I only get a little drunk. But I don't feel such apprehension. Perhaps if I got drunker, stoned, and perhaps if I felt nearer death, I'd feel differently.

31 March 2010

I watch the world pass from the train, and the passing birds. It all seems to me good. As if my relationship to death is never in terms of the world's evil – as if I'd be well out of it. No, on the contrary, if I'm *all right* out of the world at all, it's because the world seems good. In other words, I can accept and enjoy the world as it goes without me. I can take it as a world, with or without me. I'm in that mood.

The new bad news. Strangely, it can feel like an improvement. What changed? Before I was surviving, and living in fear. Now I'm in danger again, and living in hope. So it seems that the future view, rather than the present state, can be decisive.

Yes, this is possible. Or it's another way of self-cheering. But I forget. I was of course living in hope before, too. I was hoping that I was living in a sequence of good scans much longer than it proved. So each time I find a way to hope.

And hope – is it good or bad? This ambivalence about hope. Hope finally disappointed will bring greater grief: so resist it. Or hope denied is folly, even at the risk of delusion, if it brings advantage – happiness for now, or conceivably a longer life. For hope is not delusion, anyway. It doesn't claim to know. It simply wants. Respect it.

But in fact I don't feel, or not yet, that my happiness is a matter of hope. There is fear. There are blows of fear. And

I drum up hope. But this does not much alter my happiness. Not yet.

Perhaps this means that the surface of my hope hasn't really been scratched. (Being so strongly impervious, or in denial about my danger.) When it is, will I learn what it is to hold on to hope?

An email from a friend, offering one of those things I hate: a magic book against cancer. The usual remedies and diets, exercises and meditations. Nature's way. Well, should one be so abrupt in one's rejection? What do I know? On the other hand, I know that I strongly resent this. I resent not only that I have this assault upon my life, but that I'm also being asked to change my life and my self, in order to save my life; and I particularly resent the idea that nature's way might work, but I would still refuse it, and prefer an earlier death, rather than take these orders. And my objection is that it has the form of magic. I side with western medicine because it treats me as an organism. (True, this is itself partly a 'belief' of mine, about human nature, and only partly about facts.) But my refusal also allows me to continue as I have lived before, in some ways, as long as I can. So I might die for stubbornness and laziness, for a reluctance to take a risk and a little inconvenience, and I might recognise that, and still be willing, and think myself an idiot, but still not change. I hate the idea of this book because it visits me, on top of everything else, with the language of blame. Or is it the language of need?

I don't know much about hope. But it seems to me now that there is the kind of hope that includes a belief as to what is possible. There is another kind of hope that is simply desire, want, need, with no belief. And there is base hope, and to give that up is to give up everything. To lose the first or the second may lead us to lose the third also – or it may not.

Talking to Marion. In this new situation, do I have the right attitude? At my last meeting with Lucy she said that I was doing amazingly well. In what way? My attitude. I am not at all despondent. I'm amazingly undespondent. Well, this is true. Our friends say the same, M says the same, I say the same, and it is not a guard that drops when I am alone. (I have fear. I have sadness. These things I do keep to myself, to an extent. But my good spirits are not simulated.) Still, I would not describe this as an attitude. And I certainly wouldn't see it as an attitude to my illness. Perhaps it may have some effect of my illness, perhaps not. It seems to be simply how I live, how *I* live, and how I am to live: but it's not a defensive measure, rather it is a kind of duty, a duty to myself and others, not to be cast down. And it isn't a struggle.

*

'I'm going to beat this one.' I don't say that, the language of battle I reject, partly for Susan Sontag reasons, partly because they gave us to understand, from the diagnosis, that I wasn't going to beat it. A glioblastoma multiforme will come back, and sooner or later fatally. This is the thing that will kill me. Perhaps it was wrong for us to take this advice as sound, to take my limited span as the given of whatever else we do now. Another person might have rejected that warning utterly, as a passive acceptance, and adopted a determination 'to beat this one', to research whatever possible measures might help, and remain concentrated every minute, with mental focus and resolve, upon this struggle. We haven't. Perhaps because my danger is not so close (or so I fancy), I don't look to other sources of help. I prefer to rely on the efficiency of experts. On the other hand, though I know the figures roughly, I know that they can vary, so I don't think about expectations. That, I agree, wouldn't be 'helpful'.

As for trying to live better: we adopt a version of Pascal's Wager, and perhaps a better bet. Diet, exercise. It might or might not make a difference, but you won't lose much if it makes none, and it will do you some good anyway.

A lot of the time I live as if I am fine, getting on with pleasures, duties, normal things, and neglecting or overlooking my danger – with how much purpose or instinct I can't tell, to keep myself feeling good in the present. A lot of the time I am conscious of my danger, and dwelling on it, and thinking about the various ways I'm thinking about it – which perhaps is something that distracts me from directly facing it.

But NB. Just lately, now and then, I've had a sense of something I might call nausea; that is, the symptom of radical fear; that is, I may be beginning really to believe in my death; the fear of fears; this is the evacuating fear, that empties all self-strength, and sends you into any wild hope, or despair. That I would dearly be spared. Saved.

And I feel that some taking of conscious measures may be needed soon, and that my pride in my native confidence and independence won't serve. Look to externals: the world, work, love, other parts of my mind; look at them as externals to me, allowing escape into them. Or forgetting. The boy-registrar I saw a few appointments ago, said: put it out of your mind. Not such a fool. Or the travails themselves may absorb it. Or it all simply gets too exhausting. The self-mercy of the creature kicks in.

1 April 2010

I want to stop writing for a while. I am written out. Calmed down.

Perhaps I couldn't believe in any version of Christianity. Perhaps I could believe in the C of E service for the Burial of the Dead, 1662. *I know that my Redeemer liveth ... I shew you a mystery ... In the midst of life ...* It has resurrections, but – sticking to its wording – it never leaves the surface of the earth. That is where we go on living. It is a great affirmation of life on earth. And I've never been a flyer; that would be more than enough.

2 April 2010

It seems there are three attitudes, in fact. From the beginning I had no question as to which one was mine, so that the other ones didn't cross my mind.

1 To face the inevitable when it should come, trusting medicine, hoping for the best, recognising the goodness of my life as long as it might prove to be.
2 To do everything possible to prolong my life, to pursue every path, to concentrate all my thoughts upon this object.
3 To fill my time with real pleasure and new and intense experience – the round-the-world trip, the last hurrah, or whatever; I'm going to enjoy it.

The first, as I say, was always mine. And whenever the second arose, I rejected it, resented it, felt chid by it: why are you not doing all that you could possibly be doing? To which I answer: because I'm not going to count my death as a personal failure. As for the third, it was a response to a fixed sentence, a more fixed term than I've thought I had – and besides, what kind of experience could compensate for the shortening of your normal life itself? But then, that kind of experience has never been the point of my life.

But *all* those attitudes, whichever I choose, affirm only my life, my death. And against that, a universal religion affirms (at least) the common life and death of the world. That is in its favour.

> May the Lord God
> And his creation
> Be magnified.
> In dissolution
> Nothing is lost
> But the sea-level
> Has risen fast
> Against the sea wall.
>   *Alice Goodman*

4 April 2010

Easter. At M's parents' 50th anniversary gathering in Yorkshire. We go to York Minster. I take Holy Communion. (For the last time?) This collectivism is good.

5 April 2010

Easter Monday. I'm thinking on the motorway. We are inexhaustible. We have no fixed lot. There is no point at which we have spent ourselves and done all we could have. At any point and every point we are disappointed.

Therefore we might as well accept any shortening. There's no particular point, which we might hold out for. ('I just need to live for that long, until I've ...') Wherever we stop, we could have done more.

Equally, for the same reason, we could demand any length, and go on demanding more. Wherever we stop, we can do more.

So we could be satisfied with less and less, even for a mere grain of life – or we could be satisfied with nothing less than infinity. It's only a matter of degrees of disappointment.

On the motorway. We pass a traffic sign:

DELAYS POSSIBLE UNTIL 2013

I'm looking at a date that very likely I won't see.

Operation 2

6 April 2010

I'm in high excitement.

My friend's book arrives in the post, which depresses me. I skip through it. A clean American doctor. Nuts and berries, etc. The wise, sane end of nutty therapy. I'll probably read it. Diet looks OK. But if I start doing it now, I should have done this from the start, no? If I refuse now, is it out of consistency, stubbornness, too-lateness?

Then there's a phone call from Lucy, a day earlier than she said. She talks to me and to Marion. She is pleased. Mr Kitchen, the surgeon, has looked at the scans. He thinks he can operate. The tumour is growing outwards, not inwards. He thinks he can remove more, and then possibly implant some slow-release chemo in the tumour base. 'This is something we can do now.' Technically? Or they now have permission? I didn't ask. Lucy emphasises again to M that

101

this is good news. I'm an exceptional case. I have already lived longer than expected. (Did I feel that? That that's what's they thought? Not exactly.) Of course it is our decision. We have a meeting with Kitchen on Friday. (Today is Tuesday.)

For this, I'm in high excitement. It means action. It means courage. We go into the garden. My previous deep resistance to any operation is abolished in a wink. I feel this is the better path. I had a sense, about the likely new course of chemo – well, not very much was expected of it, a long and heavy procedure that might do little good. I can't work out in retrospect whether this turn-up is a surprise, or whether I thought it was more likely than I was saying. But I didn't welcome it, certainly, in advance, as I do with its arrival.

We go into the park with Eugene. The spring day and spring air is fresh and beautiful. E is packed with life, unstoppable, prodding, examining, collecting, banging, charging around, driving M half mad with his uncontrollability. M is in bewilderment with this new change, so soon after the last one; and in fear, me under the knife again, what will survive of me; the hours, as before, as she waits while I'm unconscious. Will I be as lucid after, as I was after the previous time? I don't have this fear. I trust the experts. Obviously, the question is: which procedure will give me the longer life, compos mentis? We won't feel sure that we're in a position to make this choice. But at this moment I look ahead.

*

I think that loss of speech, and of understanding of speech, and of understanding of writing, and of coherent writing, these losses will amount to the loss of my mind. I know what this feels like, and it has no insides, no internal echo. Mind means talking to oneself. There wouldn't be any secret mind surviving in me.

7 April 2010

The appointment with Kitchen at Queen Square at 9 a.m. on the 9th is booked.

Lucy said I have lived longer already than they expected. An ambiguous compliment. I think it's meant to make me feel optimistic, a good candidate for further treatment. But it could make me feel that I've already had my due.

9 April 2010

We see Neil Kitchen at Queen Square, first appointment of the morning, spry, lithe, in blue scrubs, one marked N, the other K, slightly warmer this time, but still mysterious and impersonal, really only interested in where his expertise overlaps with my troubles, very uninterested in my symptoms; which only strengthens my belief in his expertise. He shows that it is simple. The tumour has not grown inward, deeply into the brain. It has grown back where it was, peripherally, directly behind the window of bone that he had removed before. We can see this on the scan. It is logical to remove it. Lucy will then take over the chemo. He's not interested, it turns out, in the idea of an implant; doubtful of its effect, and it might be sloshing around the cavity; Lucy has agreed. When would we like the operation? How about Tuesday? (This is Friday.) We say yes, go ahead. He explains that he has a free slot. He says: we'll take you in on Monday. There's nothing more to discuss. We are through in 20 minutes. We're taken along to pre-admissions, have blood and other tests, questionnaire, and out. And now I'm going to have this enormously expensive operation, with a wait of four days, for nothing. The National Health. The nation, fighting for my life!

My father may well die while I'm in hospital.

It's another beautiful day. We drive down with E and friends to the south coast to see an art show.

Seeing the tumour on the scan, I realise that I never personify it, or think of it as an agent or as an enemy. I don't really visualise it as a solid presence (lump) or an area of events (growing). I can vaguely locate it. But it is just an abstract process, which has some effects on me – language –

and which will sooner or later kill me, but can be prevented to an extent. The way in which it has recently started to grow, operably again, is pure luck. Of course, if it gave me pain, everything might be different. But the brain has no sensations, and my tumour hasn't caused any headaching skull pressure.

It's after midnight. It's Eugene's third birthday.

10 April 2010

Another summer day. It makes me think of the endless summers of childhood; and of the summer of 1976 when I went walking to Glastonbury with my donkey Amos.

M is full of fears about how I'll come out of the operation. I'm not. But of course I could be killed or brain-damaged. All these remote dangers are possible.

11 April 2010

Eugene's birthday party too. A great party for him and us. Pleasure and food and help from friends. Tomorrow we expect hospital. Tonight we go to bed.

12 April 2010

It is night. I'm looking back over the day. M has come in with me, then collected E from nursery, then left him (upset, briefly) with Kathy and again come in. Various preparations. One doctor incompetently fixes a lead into a vein, for the third time. Knobs are stuck onto the head. Down to the MRI scan, after some hanging around. M back now. A new registrar arrives; arrogant, inattentive, supercilious.

We stand, holding each other in one another's arms, out on the stairs' landing. These times when you could go on for ever, or you could part now, you don't know which: that's to say, you're saying goodbye. Goodbye again.

I sit down on the bed and go to sleep quickly at 9.30. I'm woken at 1 a.m., someone wanting to test my reflexes. I'm awake. There's a night sonata in the ward: intermittent beeps, signals, respirators, distant phone calls, soft snoring, at various speeds – like the insect nocturne in Bartok's 3rd Piano Concerto.

Now I begin lightly fretting. I can't properly remember how my articulacy worked after the previous times. I spoke well, to start with. I wasn't allowed to use my laptop. I peeped at it to check email. Could I write? Poems slowly came back to me, line by line. I can't recall poems now, haven't been able to do this for some time, it's gone from me gradually over the last year – is that right? Or quite lately? Recently, I think, with the return of the tumour. I can only get phrases out here and there, though the rhythm remains OK. What next?

M is right to say we haven't been tested. Our steady happiness: how strong will it prove? I don't know if any of my thoughts of death, up to this day, will amount to anything. It seems to me there's a dimension around the corner I haven't yet had a glimpse of. Will it be this year?

With E: I have tried to keep my distance, I know, so he wouldn't be too dependent on and attached to me, and me being there. Stupid, and impossible anyway now: we are in the thick of one another. Though he will, I'm sure, recover from my death.

But M: you asked for a love letter. Have I ever written you one? I remember, at the beginnings of us, we were very cautious of the word, even though it seems so obvious to say it, still we feared we might suddenly irresponsibly jump into it, and get stuck in falsehood – at least, we were consciously avoiding it, when we mightn't have. Your cue, your carefulness: another case of your wisdom. And then in getting us to get married, you managed through a process of joking – 'shall we get married?' – joking, joking, until it became inevitable. And then into getting us to have a baby – 'it would be such fun' – until somehow, I can't remember how, I was overcome. It all came true. And now all I want is: prolong, prolong – though of course an open-ended life would suit us so much better. Now I should go back to sleep. I send you all my love from the middle of the night. Hold on to me. Hold on to us.

13 April 2010

I woke before 6 a.m. A few more notes, as usual about
mortality, revising, refining, rather pointlessly. Still, perhaps the story is actually simple enough. OK, true, on the
one hand, not rapidly ending and making a finish; and on
the other not finally overcoming it, and leaving the story
behind. But prolongation is also a familiar narrative
form. There is the cliff-hanger serial. There is the
shaggy-dog. The soap-opera. The tale is spun out, with an
ending wanting to be endlessly deferred. My diagnosis
belongs to a low or middle genre. Prolong, prolong.
Scheherazade – except that the conclusion is known ahead
to be different.

Mr Kitchen comes to the bed. I say, whatever else, I need
my language. He's aware of this. Then lovely anaesthesia.
I awake in recovery, 11 a.m., moving, speaking, being
constantly asked for the month, year, place, and made to
do simple exercises. Things go very badly for M, who is
trying to get through, and some idiot tells her that I will
be in theatre until 4 p.m. – something that makes no sense
in fact, but she fears that the operation has gone horribly
wrong. In recovery they've managed only to have her
landline, where she isn't of course. By 1 p.m. I insist that
they get both our mobile numbers from my bedside, and
a nurse rings her, and I can hear that she half-collapses on

the phone. Finally she gets into recovery for a brief embrace.

Back in the ward. Six beds. Visitors. Sleep. Every other man here seems to be half-dead. Groaning, gasping, faintly moaning, gurgling.

14 April 2010

Earlyish morning. The arrogant registrar arrives. Have I had any further unusual smells? I have had no unusual smells at any point. (Where does he get these ideas?) I suggest that he must be thinking of another patient. He smiles and goes.

Today my speech and writing is becoming not so fluent. Though I do make some notes about pictures and other things. Several visitors. Books. Radio. Food.

And today both M and E have gone down with bugs, and can't come in, nor for rest of the week.

15 April 2010

Some symptoms.
    They happen intermittently, but together, like this:

1 My right hand has a strange feeling of slime on my palm, and also a slight scratching; of course, this is only how it feels; it's an illusion. When I touch it with my left hand fingers, they don't register any clamminess.

2 My ability to speak and write is lost, temporarily, to some extent.

Then, after a while, these things recede; the sensation of clamminess passes very quickly, language comes back more slowly. Is this slimy hand an aura, coming ahead of a speech fit?

A fit, briefly in the morning, at say 10 a.m.

Another, in the evening, for a longer period, after 7 p.m. My friend, Dr Matt Parton, a neurologist, who works at this hospital, happened to be visiting me at that very time, and added some notes to my notes.

In the middle of the night, I woke, and shortly afterwards it happened again, at roughly 4.30 a.m.

Again, very briefly at, say, 8.15 a.m.

16 April 2010

The arrogant registrar. I tell him my symptoms. He explains that I am very lucky to have any speech, given where the operation occurred; that's all. I can of course imagine that he might disagree with Kitchen's ability/determination to preserve my language. What disgusts me is his smug indifference, his total lack of professional concern for the patients in his care.

These disruptions the previous day have some after-effects through the next day. I am trying to take measures, meanwhile, because I find that although my speaking is working automatically, I can't easily translate this speaking into my writing. I cannot grasp, in my mind, the words I'm using. I have no idea of their spelling, or articulating syllables, or making out of sounds. Or rather, it can take ages, going over and over, to work out a word. Anything that has complicated phonemes, stress or length is difficult. So I start to make a list of words that I might use very commonly, and want to have them there ready for the next time they slip away. I'm not sure this will actually work. But because I have started this list, I haven't totally lost spelling.

I should also say that the problems work vice versa. I can be talking to someone, and I have a word in mind that I want to say, and it is impossible to pronounce it properly. 'Diplomacy' was one today. Blocked. I had a go, over and over, and had to leave it. Every time, it got an 's' in the middle of it, and the stress jumped around within it. ('Diplomat' was much less trouble.) Yet the spelled word, envisaged in my mind, was perfectly clear, and I wrote it out easily. The speaking solution here is sometimes not to be slow, careful, not trying, but running at it swiftly, casually, and it will come out fluently.

A visit from a neurologist in the evening. All very friendly. She knows Matt. She actually lives round the corner from us. I'm occupying a nice little bourgeois corner in this ward, with my larder full of tasty food. I can go tomorrow.

17 April 2010

Mr Kitchen turned up this morning with a big sweet little smile (first time) and gave a small funny shrug/flap-out of his arms and then a pat on my shoulder. I think he is an angel.

Discharged. M and E are both still infectious, and I can't see either of them so I am picked up, and go to friends in Dulwich. Miserable, in one way; very good recuperation on the other hand, in a very peaceful large catered house in beautiful weather, sleeping well.

18 April 2010

A couple of times, during the weekend, after doing some writing, I have the aura feeling in the right hand. But this is not followed by any loss of language. It happens while I'm writing an email to M:

'Now listen – I believe that I'm about to have another fit, at this moment, while I'm writing to you. At least, I now have this clammy sensation in the right hand, which is my new aura (have I mentioned that?). How annoying. Don't worry.

'Or rather, apparently, no. I keep writing, speaking aloud, and I don't seem to be having any accompanying symptoms of speech/writing loss, as I did a couple of days ago. And the clammy palm has now passed. So this "aura" wasn't presaging anything. Odd. Everything continues.'

19 April 2010

M and E now well enough. M picks me up. When she brought E home from nursery, for a while he refused to look at me or talk to me, while at the same time he was playing right next to me. Then he invited me to play. It was very touching.

9 May 2010

Several weeks have passed. These intervals of calm, vacancy, have happened before. I am in a happy-ish state. There are no recurring speech fits. I'm feeling generally well. The weather has been beautiful. Eugene flourishes, full of happiness, growing. I really don't have much to say. My father's funeral is on 29 April. The next day, an appointment with Lucy. She decides to repeat the same chemo as before, at the same dosage: five days per 28. Then the weather worsens. M is miserable – still in shock from the operation, anxious for E's ear infection, gloomed by my self-centredness. Try to talk, she says, say more what's going on in me.

The General Election.

But I can now remember little of what's been going on in my mind. I have emerged well enough from the operation. I can write OK. I notice that I'm getting clear steroid effects:

1 Initial strengthening, with perhaps hints of weakening too.
2 Extreme constant greed.
3 Patterns of waking (morning and late night) and feeling sleepy (p.m. and evening).

My speech is affected accordingly, and I am noticeably full of mistakes when reading aloud, during bedtime reading to E. Tomorrow the chemo starts. I hope it won't make me feel sick. It didn't much last time.

10 May 2010

I vomited – the first day – about two hours after taking the pills, all over the stairs. Preceded by a spate of sneezing.

12 May 2010

No further vomiting. But a small fit this morning, preceded by a clammy feeling in the right hand, and then a brief minor loss of speech. Why? I've no idea.

19 May 2010

'It's very bad luck.' Have I finally got the obvious point, as Lucy raised it, all those months ago? Somebody will get this tumour. Anyone can. Somebody must. People do. We are all in the lottery. (We are all in numerous lotteries.) But this particular lottery has very few winning tickets. It's very bad luck when it's you.

My previous dimness had been that I had seen myself as simply getting this fate out of nowhere. In which case, no question of luck arises. But seeing myself as always part of a lottery, like everyone else, perhaps makes more sense. Or at any rate, an equal sense. My lot had simply been drawn.

But if so, should I feel especially resentful? If you got a

more common killer, would that be less aggrieving? Or more? Not such bad luck?

Or to put that in another way.

Lucy: 'Considering you are so unlucky, you're doing very well.' (!)

You're so lucky, to be living so long (given your expectations)/You're so unlucky (given what normal expectations should be).

Or:

You should be dead, and you haven't yet died/You should be dead already, and you're not.

I say: I don't feel so bad, because I really do live in the present. Yes, for quite a lot of the time, I do – as I always did. Simply not believing in the future. Whereas for Marion, she lives more in the future, and with disasters constantly awaited and pressing. She can't keep these things out of her mind. I find it somehow natural that there should be this difference between our feelings. But I can't really account for it, or understand it.

Laura says, on the train back from Liverpool: you have always, from the beginning, very clearly defined and controlled how you lived. Her example: not looking things up on the net. True, I guess.

12 June 2010

The operation was 13/04. Two months ago. Initially, I came out of it very well – much more so than the first time. But gradually, or perhaps rather suddenly, my speech and writing have declined. I am losing my hard-won fluency, with various aphasic glitches again. My language is not so wild as it was in the spring. But is it more ruined? When I talked with Francis Spufford I was saying that it was a struggle to maintain my perfected fluency. And when I went to Cambridge and saw Eric I was talking about various aphasia glitches. Of course I have had these problems throughout the last year and more. But they seem more serious now – I mean, ignoring when my tumour was growing again. Are they becoming worse? And does this mean my tumour is growing again, again?

Lucy said, at my last meeting, that the brain is likely to swell, and not immediately.

I note that my problems are especially bad in the daytime; or rather, that my speaking and writing and reading are better later, after 10 p.m., and I can keep going until 3 a.m. or 4 a.m. I have associated this previously with steroids.

The symptoms are mainly these:

That I cannot summon up the necessary words.

That I cannot correctly pronounce words – though sometimes I can write down words, but can't pronounce them.

Or alternatively, I can speak correctly and fluently, but I cannot understand the words that I am saying; I can't write them down; I can't master their phonemes; or, at any rate, it takes ages to get them right, and at first I simply draw a blank. And often it is the simple words that are the most difficult.

14 June 2010

The problems with my typing seem to be worse.

The letters come out wrong: I always miss out the first letter of a word; and after that, the letters come in the wrong order, or with replacements, and have to be rewritten all the time. So these go very slowly.

And as before, but more thoroughly, the writing fails to materialise. That is, simple phrases can form in my mind, and in my voicing, and could be spoken aloud if necessary – and as before, these phrases make perfect sense, and would be understood and transcribed by others – but I cannot turn them into written forms. They come out quite automatically. They often happen at the start of a sentence. And I can even tell what I am saying, sort of: I can acknowledge the basic phatic or rhetorical functions of these phrases (affirmation, negation, concession, qualification, querying, hypothetical). But I can't grasp their specific sense. And I can't identify the letters, the words, the breaks between them, the phonemes, or how they can be analysed in their meanings. I have to work through them, repeating them over and over, to make them understood to myself, trying to speak them very slowly, hearing their consonants and noises. People would find it very odd, to be asked: what am I actually literally saying? As I say, it's the very basic expressions that elude me. 'Of course, what I'm saying …' 'Now, I have …' 'But we're all …' 'What do you …' 'If I asked someone …' They take ages. Other difficulties get worse: reading aloud, for example, reading Eugene's stories or reading my own articles; factual articles are easier to read than argumentative pieces. Grammar becomes more difficult.

24 June 2010

Recent things.

Wednesday 16/06. I went to Newcastle, to stay with Vince. M and E came up on Friday. We came back to London on Monday.

Thursday 17/06. In the evening I had a fit, like an old one. I briefly lost proper use of my right hand. Longer loss of speech. I was at home with Vince. I had a brief rest. Quite soon I was able to write to M on email. I decided the next day not to up the Epilim.

Monday 21/06. I had another fit, while in bed. It woke me up from sleep. My hand was violently shaking and it seemed completely out of control for a while, then subsided. My speech seemed unaffected, but then it was. I lay calmly and slept a bit more. I was sleeping on a sofa in the living room. I slowly recovered myself. I decided to take an extra 200mg that morning. But back in London that evening I decided not to take a further 200mg. (I had been trying to get into contact with the neurologist Dr Howard but without success, before the recent fits, because of my occasional auras and clammy palm. But anyway, the neuro in the hospital said I could up the Epilim if I felt it was needed.) I have had no more fits so far.

Tuesday 22/05. I had also felt, and rather suddenly, pains in my muscles in my arms and legs. On that morning it was hard to go down the stairs, no more than a step at a time, which I assumed was an effect of the steroids; a negative effect kicking in. But at the same time, I felt I needed a higher dose of the steroids to repair my speech deficiency. The treatment contradicts itself. Lucy had suggested that I was getting post-op brain swelling. I had sent Lucy an email on the previous Monday evening.

'I need more steroids, because I have nearly run out – I've been taking 2mg each day, and I have only 8 days left. What should I do?

'After my previous operation I was on a higher dose. And when we met last time, I mentioned that my speech incompetence was worse. So shouldn't my dose be higher again? I think it would help my talking and writing.'

She replied, that morning, 'Need to get more dex from GP. Try increasing dex to 4mg for a few days to see if this improves speech but it may not and I can review when I see you next. Have you been sent a scan date?'

On Tuesday p.m. I got a prescription from my GP at Herne Hill, and had a double dose. This evening I took an extra 2mg.

Wednesday, new doses:

Morning
Epilim: 500mg + 200mg + 200mg (= 900mg)
Steroids: 2mg
Vitamin C: 1,000mg

Evening
Epilim: 500mg + 200mg (= 700mg)
Steroids: 2mg
So: Epilim per day = 1,600mg; steroids per day = 4mg

Wednesday: my legs and arms are painful. On the other hand, my speech seems to be somewhat improved. I'm speaking better. I have better vocabulary. I'm writing a bit better. Strange, if it should have such a quick effect. And likewise today.

Now, Thursday, the day I'm writing, my muscles seem to be slightly less painful!

29 June 2010

Now my muscles are ever better. But my speech is worse again, or at any rate returning to the previous state of fluctuation. I had a scan at the weekend. We're going to see Kitchen tomorrow morning. It is perhaps simply a post-op meeting, which would have occurred anyway. I don't know what report, if any, we expect.

The days are very hot, even late at night. My feelings are kind of bored. My thoughts are hard to grasp. No contents. No reflections. That is, large parts of my days lack clear enough language to manage these thoughts. I don't get sufficiently articulate until late. It's not too bad at the moment, in fact (after 10 p.m.). But I'm still without focus, or indeed, motivation. No doubt things will quicken me tomorrow.

30 June 2010

Wrong. Kitchen wasn't in, nor were there any results available.

In company with my friend Mark W for lunch yesterday, I said: 'Talking used to be such fun. Once it was off the cuff, ad lib, spontaneous. Now, it is such a struggle.' My conversation is at best, fully plotted and planned. But I haven't quite lost it for the time being. I am still speaking. There are my written words, and my typing, and I still do all my work. So obviously I am thinking, however slow.

I can do a to-and-fro conversation, especially after warming up for half an hour. I can do it better if it's just me and one other, a friend in the morning of the day, though it is much better in the late night, when of course it's very difficult for friends to be there, except for Marion.

I can write from 10 p.m. to 2 a.m. and sometimes to 4 a.m., and the lost spelling isn't too bad. Meanwhile, Marion helps me. She writes out the words that I can't spell. Or she points out the alphabet, letter by letter.

My writing in the late hours: it is very slow, but it works. I like writing, it still remains a pleasure, but now is a struggle.

The mystery of summoning up words. Where are they in the mind, in the brain? They appear to be an agency from nowhere. They exist somewhere in our ground, or in our air. They come from unknown darkness. From a place we normally don't think about.

'To see a landscape as it is when I am not there . . .' *Simone Weil*

*

For me, no word comes without prior thought. No sentence is generated without effort. No formulation is made automatically. I am faced practically and continually with a mystery that other people have no conception of, the mystery of the generation of speech. There is no command situation, it goes back and back and back. Where the self lies at the heart of the utterance – the speaker generating the word – is always clouded. This is true for everyone but for most people this is not something to think about, the generation of words is automatic. For me that automatic link is broken. Word generation involves strain, guesswork, difficulty, imprecision.

2 July 2010

We saw Lucy. And now it seems quite possible that my tumour is growing again. The speech problems may be a sign. The scan suggests this. We will be given more definite evidence in a few days – from Kitchen and from a radiologist. But the likely result: a need for a different course of chemo, heavier, and presumably worse. So I'm feeling as if my life is beginning to be limited. Of course there are further measures, and yet further measures. There is even talk of more surgery – so soon after the last one – though unlikely, I think. But I believe that I'm out of my long lucky period. From now on, it will be only one more go, and then another one, briefer and briefer, until it fails.

And on the other hand, I have suffered very little, so far, either in my treatment or in simple physical pain. There is more to come. So my idea of calm endurance is really nothing. Before, I used to survive in the present because the reality of it simply didn't face me. Sorry.

And immediately, my optimism, my drive, returns to me again, for no encouraging reason, except that it is my life, my self. 'Simply the thing I am shall make me live.'

Slight increase of Epilim.

Morning
Epilim: 500mg + 200mg + 200mg (= 900mg)
Steroids: 2mg
Vitamin C: 1,000mg

Evening
Epilim: 500mg + 200mg + 200mg (= 900mg)
Steroids: 2mg
So: Epilim per day = 1,800mg; steroids per day = 4mg

3 July 2010

But why are we not mad?

At the moment, I don't know whether I feel normal or not. I go one way and another.

After the last operation I emerged so well. I felt confident. And the repeated treatment was offered, and it would work as before, as I imagined, for a good while. But now it's changed. It doesn't seem to have been working. Which makes me feel that the prospect of further treatment looks worse, too – more painful, or anyway more useless.

Yet I also believe that I'm a committed liver – for what else? And so, after another bout of bad news, I'm imagining another recovery. And then another. In other words, I have a way of not believing in this failing. It's as if my danger is no worse than *risky*. The bad news will arrive sooner or later – but somehow I will go on recovering. That is: there are still treatments, and then more treatments. And this is what is mentioned, of course, for now. This is what we can do. We focus only on the short-term treatments. But clearly there are limits. For example, part of the complex tumour can be treated, for a bit, but part of it starts resisting all treatment. So when might the final recognition arrive?

So that is one way of understanding my coming down. More immediately, I have always felt well, despite my abstract doom. But now I don't feel well – in the sense that my speech and the power of my mind are largely beyond me. I can't help myself, and I can't achieve it through willpower or concentration. It is simple inability. It's different from after my first operation – then it was slowly getting better, while now it is getting worse.

126

I do not even notice that I can't read most of the time. Or rather, I can manage only the simplest words and constructions, and very slowly. For example: I have lost my specific recall of passages, that is, all my poems, all my lyrics – partly gradually lost to radiotherapy, I think. Of course I know where to look things up, which is something. They are in books and in CDs. I know where they are on the shelf.

But the present obvious fact is this: I fear a new form of unpleasant treatment, and I fear that the treatment won't work anyway.

This is 2 a.m., when I am almost competent. But the writing and the vocabulary is still very unhappy.

6 July 2010

It is four months since the last bad news. And the bad news has appeared again. Or rather, it hasn't really gone away. There was the interval, the operation, that looked good. The tumour was cut out. The repeat chemo was applied. But the tumour itself has continued to grow, and the chemo has not abated it. Or that is likely.

Lucy said we'd know more this morning. For some reason, the scan has failed to get to Kitchen. Tomorrow we hope to hear it.

Meanwhile, my orientation now feels different. Perhaps it's the uncertainty still that makes this a nullity. But before,

I have always found – among other things – that my self restores itself. I had in me this comic spirit of immortality. Now I feel nothing, though perhaps this will return. At any rate, my sense of detail, fact, is very weak. My circumstances are simply abstract. I don't have enough vocabulary to grasp more. It's beyond me. Well, this is the day. The night is better. Last night I felt that my speech and my mind were in more command. I had a wider survey and a richer world. But then I'm also more tired.

And tonight at supper, more talkative, more drunk, I saw things differently again. I recognise that I am in helplessness, and I can accept this. This is part of my condition. It is not courage or strength or endurance, but nor is it totally fallen down. But this helplessness is a limited state. I continue to live through it. Meaning that this state, though of course it is only for a restricted time, need not be absolutely my single experience. I am in some ways helpless. And recognising that, I can also live outside of this helplessness too.

7 July 2010

No news again. Felt helpless, dejected. I've no idea what to expect.

All I can say is that speech failure casts all failure upon me.

At the moment I feel torn between pictures: the role of surviving, and the role of dying. Both of these roles have a self. I can hope to extend my life for a little longer, and I can recognise that my ending is in prospect. They have the same length, of course. Only their attitudes alter. And this is a different thing from last night.

Today I can write very slightly in the middle of the day (having written very late the night before). Then in the afternoon it's hopeless. Then I'm more capable from 10 p.m. on. But of course these things are very poor. My verbal capacities are very slow, limited, simple, inaccurate, non-recognitive. The mad thing is, I do get much better very late. I can go on till about 4 a.m. It seems absurd, but I feel I could push on further, and do better, though I'm tired also, of course, but excited, to have the ability again, a bit of it anyway.

Reading seems to have given up entirely. I listen to people on the radio, and I cannot repeat their words, nor can I grasp their points, but I can sort of recognise the articulations that are being made; they're there, beneath the surface. And at some time, I suspect, my speech will simply fail. Or rather, it will fail first of all at one competence, and then at another.

I want to write. I want to make plans and arguments. I want to do some reading, and look things up. I want to remodel things I've written. But my mind doesn't have these resources, though my descriptions and observations seem to be better. I am still writing. I still do all my work for newspapers. I have just written an article on Giotto's *Vices*.

Bad Again

8 July 2010

Lucy has now spoken to Kitchen. Results:

The recent chemo treatment has had no effect. (Just as well the scan was now.)

Another bout of surgery – though it is a possibility – is too recent since the last.

So there is PCV, another chemo. Beginning next week.

An appointment with Lucy tomorrow at St Thomas's. At 11 a.m.

I can have a higher dose of steroids: I will now take 2mg × 3 each day.

It comes to this. There is this new course of chemo. And after the first dose, say, it may fail to have any result, as with previous one. And then? More surgery. But even with surgery, the tumour will only increase. More chemo? Maybe. But sooner or later the tumour just gets worse. So at some point, I will start dying. And perhaps, when I look back, I will see that it has already begun. My speech problems now may signal my final fatal state.

Eugene understands that my words are going wrong, here and there. I can't sing the words of nursery rhymes. I often can't read him stories. Of course it may come back, more or less as before. Or it may decline into silence.

If I were alone, living in a wood, it might be different. I could imagine living and then dying, and be resigned. But with M and E – this is our life. And how can Eugene understand? Though he will forget, presumably.

How rapidly, finally, my tumour increases, invading everything.

But now, having said that, I look away. I'm sitting on a bench, on the ridge of the park. My writing is difficult, but I'm feeling well, in my body and (in a limited way) in my thinking. I'm not looking towards a dark future. I'm now out of this mind. The experience simply continues, until it does not. And meanwhile ... meanwhile ... well, there are troubles to be acknowledged, and there are other things to be done.

9 July 2010

Happiness. Religion and literature are often concentrated upon misery, grief, sin. These are their wisdoms. But not for me. Everything seems good.

Empson: 'I did not say he was bad because he created the world, and I think that idea a disgusting one. It is petulant snootiness to say, "The world is not good enough for me"; the world is glorious beyond all telling, and far too good for any of us.'

We have sent out again an email all round. And now this late night I am feeling full of energy and hope. How mad!

15 July 2010

I began my new chemo on 12/07. On the next day I was blotto pretty much throughout the whole day, except the evening. And the next day. I had no ability for speech for much of the day, except very late. I feel hopeless, hopeless.

I feel now that I am becoming dead. I had thought that my speech would last me for much longer. Now I am not so sure. I think that my speech is over. My mind is over. My life is over.

I need to be hard, secure, firm, solid, resolved.

Will I ever rise again?

16 July 2010

I can write a tiny little bit in the afternoon.

I noticed, when I was trying to read in the morning, it was strange. My understanding of phrases was neither with, nor without sense, but in a kind of blur, in between.

Also, there was a delay. A few minutes later I could understand what I had been reading slightly better.

But this is really nothing. In the morning it feels like this.

I don't expect ever again to write in a complicated way, or to have an articulate thought.

Everything is fading – no? Moving very quickly, coming down, against the end. But quite peaceful, too.

A sentence, a simple sentence, is about all I can do, at the moment.

So in the daytime, I cannot muster up any conversation. My language is so limited. And it makes such little joy for Marion or anyone else or indeed for me. That's why I want to say nothing at all; to remain dumb, so that my lack of speech doesn't become audible and useless.

I can put down a little more at this minute, in the afternoon. And I am writing up the brief notes I made earlier. And it seems also that I am not quite so weary after lunch. My attention grows. Is there a change, after my blotto condition on Tuesday, Wednesday, Thursday? Is it the stopping of my anti-nausea pills (which today I have left off) that have had this beneficial effect?

Of course there is still very little expansion of my vocabulary. And as for my talking, my fluency – well, we'll see. But I have managed something, in terms of writing and thinking and talking. This afternoon, I have written three very slow, short but goodish paragraphs. What next?

But much later. After 11 p.m. I have been going very fast and full. Talking, writing, reading. Volubility. An experience I haven't had for months. Will this continue tomorrow? I'm excited, but also troubled. What will happen? Will it last? I suspect that it's about the pills being dropped, plus the temporary addition of extra steroids, also now dropped. And now I can't get to sleep, even when I want to.

It's not possible to get any distance from my project: being alive. Objectively, from the outside you might say, my life is terrible, unbelievable. And it's true, I hate this. I hate the way I am at the moment. But there is no objective view, I am here, in it, and there is nothing else and this fact brings with it many things that make it of course easier. And beyond that there are many other things to think about.

25 July 2010

I want to think about writing about my life in a public form; that is, talking to this editor, and proposing my thoughts. And the thing to say is: I'm going to die. That has been sure from the beginning. How soon is not clear. A few years seems to be the idea. Ideally I would do a column. The daily little and large things are very occupying. And sometimes I can believe in it, and sometimes not. Obviously there is a problem. My crisis dates back almost two years. So there is a background that needs filling in.

28 July 2010

I send this email to Laura, to be passed to Jane F, about writing for the *Observer*:

'Dear Laura,
It strikes me that there are two ways of approaching my case, perhaps connected.

1 The starting point is a story beginning nearly two years ago, when I was told that my life would be short. I was given a diagnosis of a brain tumour, high-grade, a glioblastoma multiforme – a rare thing, and it averagely promises a two-year span. I guess for me it will be longer. I have had two operations and radiotherapies and chemos. I don't feel physically in pain at all – the brain has no nerve feelings, of course. The visible tumour is not something that I picture or personify very clearly. It is in the left temporal lobe. I can vaguely locate it from the scar.

At the same time, this life is unbelievable. At moments, it

is terrible and outrageous. But in other ways I accept what it brings, in its strangeness and newness. This mortality makes its own world. It is a mystery and many other things. And then again, I try to live as normally as I can. To be calm. To feel full. And I share my existence with my wife and our growing small son, now three, who is beginning to understand our difficulties, and we face this present and future together. Strange happiness. Never doomed. Disaster. Always extremes.

And another thing to know is that the tumour is in the region of my speech functions. At some point, they will be seriously affected. A great fear. There have been small dysphasic glitches, and brief fits, since the start. It is almost a free-standing story. But in the last two months my speech has become much more difficult, and there are times now when I think I am lost. There are several strands of deficit – reading, listening, spelling, mustering vocabulary, remembering songs. My writing and talking mainly work better late at night, for some reason – up to 4 a.m. And of course my writing is my earning. I don't know if its previous power will return. I am now at the start of a new course of chemo. At the moment, we don't know if it will work. Or failing that, what might follow.

2 I would want to write a column, now, because it needs to be told in a true way. When you get a cancer diagnosis, the story is expected to have two options. Either there is an ending, with death. Or there is an overcoming. And both are satisfactory conclusions. But prolongation, unclear survival,

is also a familiar narrative form. There is the shaggy-dog story that I and my family live in. Likewise this hope for speech. The tale is spun out, with an ending wanting to be endlessly deferred.'

Last weekend we went back to our friends, to their cottage in Suffolk. Almost two years ago, it was there my first fit happened in the middle of the night; and I was ambulanced into hospital, where it all began. We hadn't been there subsequently at all. Bad fate! And now it is our return!

But then on Sunday morning I had another fit there, quite serious, with total loss of speech, and the ambulance came out again. Fortunately, my speech returned quite soon. But it looked like another hospitalisation for a moment. Bad luck for them. Bad luck for us. We must apologise deeply. Of course it is no one's fault. But the fault is there, standing in our face! 'For it must needs be that offences come; but woe to that man by whom the offence cometh!' (Matt. 18 v. 7: a rare exclamation point in the AV, maybe? It has taken a long time trying to trace this quotation; once I could remember all these things.)

I have been only slowly recovering from this fit. But strangely, it seems that my speech is generally in a better state; that is, my morning behaviour seems rich, and perhaps in the evening too, though the early afternoon is relatively in decline, but still fluent. After all, I am writing at this moment, and spelling without going spell-blind. On the other hand, my actual speaking is poor.

30 July 2010

I would like to write in other forms, and in other ways of understanding. For example, thinking about dying and the imagining of it – it must be connected to its cultural forms, and to broader linguistic forms. But I don't address myself to these areas. Also, I literally want to adventure, rather than going again into my normal patterns of self-concentration, which are always slightly different, but not much. If it was possible to move out onto flights and into depths. And my sense of vocabulary is so poor – and the grammar too – oh, how hard it is to construct anything requiring more than a simple statement. What a struggle for me. What a boring experience for other readers. So I am mainly dedicated to regret. At this moment.

My working way. It feels more disciplined. It doesn't have inspirations, sudden flashes, going off in odd directions, diversions, forgetting what I am doing. I progress on a more single path. I follow procedure. And yet the results don't seem to be very different at the end of the day. No, because the grammar, as I have said, is so simple.

*

I am still a protagonist. Or rather, there are two of them. There is the die-er and the survivor. Both of them last for the same span, have the same future. But they have a different name.

1 August 2010

Into Guy's Hospital, for five days. Bad results.

16 August 2010

To the Mill in Norfolk. A very serious fit the following day. I'm taken into King's Lynn Hospital, for one day. Marion has to fight to get me discharged.

20 August 2010

Things are very much lost. I can't really write at all, except very late, and very limitedly.

At the moment it's only 7 p.m.

I want to think about my article: about the beginning of this life.

It was exactly two years ago. This life began with my first fit. My immediate symptom was recognised as a brain tumour – with the first operation – and the fact that my life wouldn't last very long.

My acceptance of my death. My gratitude for my medicine.

Though the future was always waiting.

And then, rather recently, there have been the growing problems with speech.

And it's very hard on my limbs.

I should have made more notes at the Mill.

24 August 2010

My thoughts – staying in life – crossing over to death – hope – despair – bored by these ideas – want to concentrate on other things – but of course also I want to stay in life – that is now clear – when before I was more twofold – now there is much to do – and my existence has plenty in it – and I like it – even though my writing is poor this late night (though the improvement in my illustration on one of my collages was good) – I feel very wakeful at the moment – I do not think myself lost.

26 August 2010

The second half of July was full of writing. I think that it was the result of the chemo and its extra steroids, and the strong fit I experienced, as well. I made a very fluent description of, and commentary about, a painting. I hope that more steroids will give me stronger effects. We will talk to Lucy tomorrow.

Jane F, editor of the *Observer*, has taken an interest in my article about my mortality. I can write four thousand words if I want to. So I have to do my best. But it is a struggle at this moment. The time is half-past eleven, and my abilities are not very good.

In this piece: how many episodes are to be involved?

How long should I have sequences of argument?

How about small quotations?

And where is the second part beginning?

And what I write about at the moment is very functional. I should like to write more rhetorical and aphoristic language.

I am a divided creature. One side makes me a hopeful survivor. (My treatment has a given future still.) The other side makes me an obvious stopper. Meanwhile, I must recognise that my mortal role is full. And can I call it a form of play? Yes. Even this is a happiness. I have not yet found this void. And perhaps so long as I can fill out this play, dying itself may be accepted.

October 2010

I can still voice words.

But I am now pre-computer again – no thesaurus, no email, no newspapers, no radio, not now even a pen.

But I find my brain is still busy, moving, thinking. I am surprised.

My language to describe things in the world is very small, limited.

My thoughts when I look at the world are vast, limitless and normal, same as they ever were.

My experience of the world is not made less by lack of language but is essentially unchanged.

This is curious.

'Would it be imaginable that people should never speak an audible language, but should still say things to themselves in the imagination?' (Ludwig Wittgenstein).

One way, but not the other way, but sometimes in both ways.

Pure music I can do, narrative music I can't.

Film, I understand shape and colour but not story.

Poetry is still beautiful, taking me with it.

Pictures, I understand abstract but not story. But I can actually do much more still with pictures. This is my job.

My language works in ever-decreasing circles, the whole of English richness is lost to me and I move fewer and fewer words around.

*

I cannot count. At all.

Marion and her embrace.
Ground, river and sea.
Eugene – his toys, his farm, his cars, his fishing game.
Getting quiet.

Names are going.

Writing, there is no voice. Or rather; writing is still there in its old form but it's gone quiet. It fluctuates and gets more difficult.

I can't understand what people say so clearly, what they mean, what they intend.
I can write, just about.
It's very difficult for me to talk at all (one way just hopes for sense and another way is total nonsense).
But all the same, it's amazing what Marion can do, how it can still happen.

First of all it was scary; now it's all right; it is still, even now, interesting.
My true exit may be accompanied by no words at all, all gone.

The final thing. The illiterate. The dumb.
Speech?

Quiet but still something?
Noises?
Nothing?

My body. My tree.

After that it becomes simply the world.